Praise for

difference

"This book is a generous work of genius. The Difference Map is now an essential component for anyone who is serious about doing work that matters, and Bernadette Jiwa is the bright new star to lead us there."
—SETH GODIN, AUTHOR OF *LINCHPIN*

"An inspiring read and a truly powerful tool. Bernadette is a rare find —she doesn't just know what she's talking about, she's not afraid to stand for why it matters. What better way to describe the challenge we all face in trying to make real connections in today's world?"
—JONATHAN RAYMOND, EMYTH, CHIEF BRAND OFFICER

"Have you wondered about that "certain something" that makes an extraordinary business? Bernadette's stylish little book is that "certain something" explained."
—MARK SCHAEFER, AUTHOR OF *RETURN ON INFLUENCE* AND *THE TAO OF TWITTER*

"Bernadette is the Banksy of the marketing world."
—MERRYN PADGETT, FOUNDER OF EARTH & SEA CREATIVE

difference

THE ONE-PAGE METHOD FOR
REIMAGINING YOUR BUSINESS AND
REINVENTING YOUR MARKETING

BERNADETTE JIWA

THE STORY OF TELLING PRESS

AUSTRALIA

Published in Australia by The Story of Telling Press.

www.thestoryoftelling.com

Portions of this book have appeared previously on
TheStoryofTelling.com blog.

Library of Congress Cataloging-in-Publication Data

Jiwa, Bernadette
difference : the one-page method for reimagining your business and
reinventing your marketing / by Bernadette Jiwa
p. cm.
1. Marketing. 2. Business Development. I. Title.
II. Title: difference

ISBN 978-1494842710

Printed in the United States of America

Book and Jacket Design: Reese Spykerman

10 9 8 7 6 5 4 3 2 1

First Edition

For my boys

Contents

difference

Introduction

THINKING DIFFERENCE

During the '70s a small team of some of the world's best computer engineers was working in Silicon Valley at PARC, Xerox's research and innovation division. Their task was to take the company's vision for the office of the future and make it a reality. Everyone who was anyone in the Valley knew that Xerox was at the leading edge of what the future would look like. These engineers were working on a bunch of things, one of which was improving upon a pointing device that was designed to be used with a computer—a pointing device that we now know as the mouse. The idea wasn't new and it hadn't been hatched by the team at PARC; the first prototype of the mouse, invented by Doug Engelbart, had actually been around since the '60s.

On a rare occasion in 1979, when a select group of visitors was invited to see what the PARC team was working on, scientist Larry Tesler demonstrated how a computer with icons on the screen could be controlled by this pointing device. It just so happened that one of the visitors that day was Steve Jobs. The story goes that as soon as he saw what would become the modern-day mouse in action, Jobs began pacing the room excitedly, and when he finally couldn't contain himself any longer, he said, 'you're sitting on a gold mine'. And 'this is insanely great'. For the life of him, Steve Jobs couldn't understand why Xerox wasn't doing anything with this invention.

While the PARC team focused on developing the product they thought the mouse would eventually become—a $300 accessory built as part of a costly business computer—Steve Jobs had other ideas. A day or two after his visit to Xerox, Jobs met with design consultant Dean Hovey

1

and told him to forget about everything else he was working on for Apple. Jobs knew exactly what they must do next.

The design brief he gave Hovey for the mouse was simple. There were just four criteria:

1. It had to be built for less than $15.

2. It had to last for two years.

3. It needed to work on a typical desktop of Formica or metal.

4. *And* it had to work on Jobs' Levi's.

It's clear that Jobs' vision from the start was that the mouse should be designed as an affordable consumer product. He had flipped the traditional product development model on its head. Instead of thinking about the features and function of the product in isolation, Jobs made a leap to consider what the product might mean to potential customers. He wasn't concerned so much with what the innovation did; he was more excited about what it would enable people to do. Now, instead of memorizing and typing long commands on a text-based screen, users could point to an icon and click or drag. Imagine the difference between typing a command like

```
move c:\clients\apple\sjobs.txt a:\billing\
invoices\sjobs.txt
```

and just dragging the file's icon to the folder you wanted to move it to.

When the Apple Macintosh was launched in January 1984, it was the first mass-market personal computer to feature a graphical user interface and a mouse. And that changed everything.

Malcolm Gladwell describes Jobs as 'a tweaker' who was 'endlessly refining the same territory he had claimed as a young man'. Others have said that he was an editor with an instinct for innovation, and not an inventor at all. But Jobs' real genius was that he had learned how to see and he operated with an understanding of and empathy for the people who would become future users of Apple products—devices like the iPad that would 'make our heart sing'. As Hovey said, Jobs 'connected the dots' and was 'brilliant at figuring out what a computer ought to be "for the rest of us"'. Steve Jobs was what I call a 'difference thinker'.

'Difference thinking' is more than the ability to connect the dots, though. It's about seeing the truth, recognising the opportunity in that truth and *then* acting on it. You need to learn how to see the dots and understand the significance of connecting them before you can begin. And you can do that only by identifying with and understanding somebody else's feelings and frustrations. That's what Steve Jobs did intuitively; he had the ability to stand in a potential user's shoes and understand the impact that an innovation and its design might have on that person's life (and thus in the market). This is something you can train yourself to do, too.

BEING DIFFERENT VS. CREATING DIFFERENCE

Business has traditionally seen innovation as something that is incremental. We constantly strive to be different from or to outdo the competition, so we build on what already exists, to either create big changes or make small improvements. We tweak, give a bit extra, or perhaps add one more feature, and then we figure out ways to get people to notice how we're different so we can convince them to buy our products and services. This thinking has led us to bring things to market in a way that looks something like this:

IDEA—> DEVELOP—>LAUNCH—>MARKET

In contrast, difference thinkers don't begin with an idea and think in increments of improvement; they start with empathy. This gives them the ability to take what is and understand what could be. The product or service that is born from creating difference in this way *is* the marketing.

An idea developed with difference thinking looks like this:

TRUTH—>PEOPLE—>IDEA—>LAUNCH

This is how the now-ubiquitous humble shopping cart was invented and adopted eighty years ago. Sylvan Goldman, a grocery store owner from Oklahoma, noticed that when his customers' baskets became too heavy or too full, people stopped shopping. Clearly their problem was his problem, too. He began to think of ways to improve the experience for his customers. In 1936 he came up with the idea of a basket carrier on wheels. The concept was developed from the simple idea of using a folding chair as a framework to carry two baskets. A year and several iterations later, Goldman launched the new 'folding basket carrier' in his stores. The strange thing was that even though it was designed to make their lives easier, customers hated the shopping cart. They didn't warm to using it at all. Men worried that they would look weak if they couldn't haul a heavy load of groceries. Young women thought that the carts were unfashionable, and older people didn't want to appear helpless by using them.

Mr Goldman was not one to give up on an idea, so he took a step back; he considered his customers' worldview and thought about what might change how people felt about using the carts. Next, he hired models of both sexes and all ages to push shopping carts around his store as if they were shopping. He also hired a friendly store greeter who would offer carts to people as they arrived, pointing out that everyone was using them. And the rest, as they say, is history.

Just three years later, the shopping cart was so cemented in American culture that it appeared on the cover of *The Saturday Evening Post,* and supermarkets were redesigned to accommodate its use.

I wonder what Mr Goldman would think if he could see the impact of his invention today. How times have changed! Now every modern man (my husband included) knows that driving the shopping cart frees you to make more impulse buys at speed when you go out to buy the forgotten milk at 8 p.m. And the shopping-cart symbol has become so universally representative of the buying experience that it's how we know we're shopping even when we're buying online with our feet up on the sofa.

We have been conditioned to believe that the way to succeed is to have an advantage, to be different or better. But what does it mean to be different? It means raising the bar, being one step ahead, standing out because you are incrementally better than the competition—at least until the competition gets a step ahead of *you.* Ultimately, though, it means being on the same page and in the same category as that competition.

Creating difference, on the other hand, is about seeing things in a whole new light. It's about re-imagining what the problem or the need might be, and then deciding that you will do whatever it takes to be the one to solve this problem for people. This approach leads to the creation of innovations and solutions that redefine the rules of the game, that reinvent a category or experience.

Through personal experience, David Gilboa, co-founder of eyewear retailer Warby Parker, understood the pain of losing a $700 pair of glasses that he couldn't afford to replace—maybe you have experienced this, too? David's co-founder, Neil Blumenthal, had previously worked with Vision Spring, a non-profit that helped people in developing countries to get access to the glasses they needed, so he understood that style mattered to even the poorest people in the world. These experiences lay at the core of David and Neil's idea to bring affordable and stylish prescription eyewear to the world.

Creating difference is not about finding a new, improved way of beating the competition. It's about reimagining what it means to *be* the competition. It's about closing the gap between what already exists and what could be. Creating difference means setting your own new bar by understanding how to fill the tiniest gap in human desire. Because difference is not just noticed; it's experienced and felt.

Do you need to have a brand new idea or invent something radically different in order to create difference? No, not necessarily. Starbucks didn't invent coffee, and Apple didn't invent the smartphone; these companies simply created new *experiences* of them, which in turn created a whole new set of meanings that we attached to what were once commodities.

Fifty years ago, the focus of business was dominance. *More* was the shortcut to becoming an unbeatable Goliath in the marketplace. Today the shortcut to *more* is to matter—not to be different, but to do something that creates difference. It isn't the person with the best idea who wins; it's the person who has the greatest understanding of what really matters to people.

being different

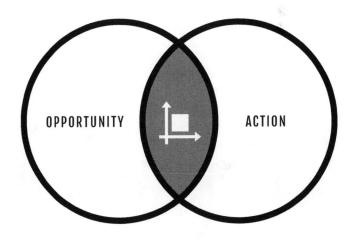

OPPORTUNITY · ACTION

creating difference

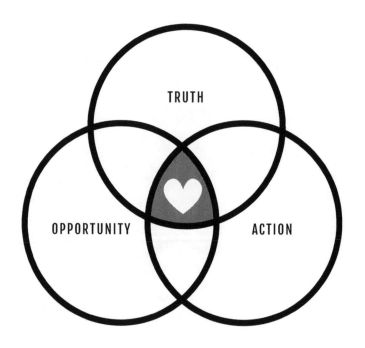

Your way forward is *not* simply to look for opportunities to be distinguishable from, or one step ahead of, the competition. Your job is *not* to find ways to be the alternative. Just like your favourite café has somehow managed to become part of your story almost without your realising it, your job is to become 'the one'. In order to do that, you need to understand the story that people want to believe and become invested in. Because the truth is that you can't change how people think or what they do without changing how they feel.

Every day I work with business owners who want to unlock the value in their brand story. Here's what I've found. You can't begin to tell a story without understanding why that story should matter to the people you want to serve. You can't build a great business just by being different. You need to create ideas and experiences that give people reasons to care and to belong, not just reasons to choose. I've decoded how the most successful brands of our time have managed to do just that, using what I call the *Difference Model*. Yes, there is a way to kickstart yourself and your organisation into thinking in terms of the difference you create, and with that in mind I've developed a template that helps you to reimagine your business and reinvent your marketing in the same way that organisations like Uber, Spanx, Apple and Patagonia have done. You'll discover the model and see it in action later in the book.

This book is your invitation to show up and bring ideas that matter to the world. It's the guidepost that will help you learn how to see and how to unlock the value in your story. It's an invitation to matter to people—your customers, readers, users and clients—so that your work can create a difference.

THE TEN CHARACTERISTICS OF
DIFFERENCE THINKERS

1. They practice empathy because they care enough to make an impact.

2. They have a clear sense of the change they want to make in the world.

3. They are impatient about tactics and endlessly patient about implementing their strategy.

4. They ask the right questions, and that means that they talk more than twice as much as they listen, because talking takes guts. Mostly, they ignore those who offer empty criticism.

5. They watch what people do and don't just believe what people tell them.

6. They innovate and create at the edges, ignoring the market of everyone.

7. They make products for their customers, instead of trying to find customers for their products.

8. They understand that they need to give people a story to tell—a 'you've gotta see this' moment.

9. They work hard to change how people feel, by creating intangible value that gives them an emotional point of difference.

10. They understand that trust is their second-most valuable asset. The first is the willingness to be wrong for the right reason.

Our Marketing-Made World

THE LOST ART OF MARKETING

If you'd lived in Europe during the medieval era, wheat and cereals would have been your staple foods. In fact, up to three quarters of what you ate would have been porridge or gruel and, later, bread. This dependence on one crop as the staple food was recognised as a problem by the aristocracy and rulers of the time. There was, however, an alternative. The potato had been cultivated in South America for centuries, but hadn't been widely adopted in Europe. Europeans were suspicious of a food that didn't smell or taste of much. The Spanish first grew potatoes mainly to feed to livestock, which was about all that most sceptical European farmers thought potatoes were good for. After all, anything that looked that ugly and misshapen couldn't be fit for human consumption. Could it?

The rulers of the day recognised the huge potential of the potato as an alternative food source, and they began to dream up ways to encourage their subjects to grow them. There were even pro-potato editorials published in *The Times*. In France it took a royal seal of approval and the sight of King Louis XVI and Marie Antoinette wearing potato flowers as decorations to tip the balance in the potato's favour.

Frederick the Great of Prussia had a challenge on his hands. He saw the potential of the potato to keep the price of bread down and to protect his people against famine. But despite trying to persuade them by using logic, and even going so far as to issue an order in 1774 for his subjects to grow potatoes, people still remained sceptical, remarking that not even dogs would eat the ugly, tasteless vegetable. Frederick had recognised the opportunity in adopting something different, but because he wasn't acting with empathy and seeing the truth through the eyes of his subjects, his argument wasn't convincing. Clearly the product wasn't selling.

It was only when he began to frame the problem with empathy, using his subjects' worldview, that Frederick had an epiphany that would change his next course of action, and history into the bargain. Frederick instructed his gardeners to plant a field of royal potatoes and then surrounded it with heavily armed guards to protect the potato crop from thieves (but not to guard it too well). The local peasants naturally assumed that anything the king thought was worth guarding must be of value, and they made it their business to get their hands on some of the royal crop so that they could plant it for themselves.

A win for Frederick, and for his people, even if they didn't know it at the time. Economists have estimated that the introduction of the potato was responsible for a quarter of the growth in Old World population between 1700 and 1900. I doubt that some of my own Irish ancestors would have existed without Frederick the Great's clever intervention.

As marketers over the past few decades, we made the mistake of forgetting to see the world through the eyes of the people we wanted our ideas to matter to. We went from operating with empathy to selfishly trying to make people pay attention to what we had to say or sell, whether they might want it or not. By looking for a shortcut to a quick win, we wasted chances to be generous, to engage with and inspire people. But in a world of infinite choices and digitally empowered consumers, quick wins no longer build sustainable businesses, and they certainly don't create brands that people care about. Now more than ever before, the ideas, businesses and brands that succeed are the ones that help to reinforce, enhance and shape the cultures, beliefs, aspirations and behaviours of their audience. Brands that have recognised and found a way to become part of subtle cultural shifts—shifts around nomadism, conscious consumption, simplicity, provenance, environmental consciousness, connectedness, self-expression, nostalgia, adventure, real food, female body image and on and on—have thrived. Examples include Lululemon, Whole Foods, Airbnb, Warby Parker, Kickstarter, Instagram, Dove, KeepCup, Patagonia, Innocent Juices, Method, Zipcar, charity: water, Dropbox, TED.com, Apple, Starbucks, Khan Academy, Task Rabbit and Sugru, to name a few.

Conventional wisdom advocates developing a product and then creating a big marketing funnel in order to sell it, which means doing whatever we can to attract the most potential customers and then to convert some to leads. The tactic is to bombard those leads with our messages in the hope of getting a few people to care about our products and services. This approach has become an unsustainable and zero-sum game. What's working now is doing exactly the opposite: figuring out what people want and finding ways to delight one person at a time, one person who is thrilled to talk about you to her friends, essentially turning the funnel on its head.

Open any business book and it will tell you that marketing is the set of activities involved in the transfer of goods from the seller to a buyer. The exchange of products for money. This for that. Even in the days before advertising, though, when ancient tribes traded pieces of flint for other things they needed, marketing was much more than a series of activities that ended in a transaction.

Actually, marketing *is*, and has always been, a transfer of emotion. It's about changing how people feel and, in turn, helping them to fall in love with something, or maybe just a little bit more in love with themselves.

Marketing has always been an art. We've tried to turn it into pure science with big data and focus groups. Of course it's helpful to be able to use analytics to know how long people spend on your website or where they give up during the on-boarding process for your application. And while AB testing will tell you which version of your landing page or copy a customer prefers, and that information is useful, too, it's not enough. In order to create the product or write that copy in the first place, you need to have a story to tell, a story that your customers will want to believe in. And before you can begin to create difference for them, you need a product or service they can care about and love using. Some of the marketing theories and practices of the past seventy years made us forget that. This is our chance to rewrite that story.

It's not just time to flip the funnel; it's time to care about what people actually want. In our digital world, customers exchange things that can be far more valuable than cold hard cash, things like time, loyalty, content, ideas and endorsements. I believe we need to change our thinking, and begin building our businesses around difference, to help our customers not just to buy from us but to love our brands because they believe in what we do.

HOW WE GOT HERE

The original Marketing Mix, using the four Ps classification, was proposed in 1965 (before many people even had a TV set) by the marketer E. Jerome McCarthy. It was a framework for considering how to grow a business and gain market share. The mix consisted of four Ps—product, price, place and promotion—a list of ingredients that marketers must pay attention to in order to ensure that their products succeeded in the market.

Over the years extra Ps were added. Ries and Trout gave us *positioning* at a time when more and more products were being brought to market. Positioning began with the product, but it wasn't what you did to the product to make it better that mattered. Positioning was all about what you did to the 'mind of the prospect'. Advertisers looked for 'holes in the marketplace' or positions their clients could own.

> *The basic approach to positioning is not to create
> something new and different, but to manipulate what's
> already up there in the mind.*
> —AL RIES AND JACK TROUT,
> *POSITIONING: THE BATTLE FOR YOUR MIND*

And it helped for a little while, in a pre-digital age when people regarded adverts as information and customers chose from limited ranges that local retailers stocked. In fact, I'm sure Ries and Trout were partly responsible for my Cadbury's Crème Egg addiction in the '70s. But in a world with seemingly infinite choices, where *customers* get to control the conversation, we need to consider a different set of Ps and a new form of marketing, a form that is no longer purely product or company focused, but one that is built on difference thinking.

IS IT TIME TO STOP ADVERTISING?

Last week I passed a kid bobbing about at the side of the road, where cars sped by at 80km per hour. He was wearing a red sandwich board that screamed, 'BUY ONE GET ONE FREE', and he had clearly been given instructions to dance about to attract more attention. I was 200 metres past him when I realised he was advertising the unremarkable pizza place on the other side of the road. The dancing-sandwich-board guy once again made me question the value of advertising.

We spent $500 billion globally on advertising in 2013. Every year we're spending more money, to interrupt more people, more often, with messages they don't care about and don't pay attention to. We've come to believe that the way to succeed is to have an advantage—by being different or better, more visible, or just plain louder.

Advertising by definition was never designed to deliver either value or joy.

> **advertise (verb)**
> 1. to announce or praise (a product, service, etc.) in some public medium of communication in order to induce people to buy or use it: to advertise a new brand of toothpaste.
> 2. to give information to the public about; announce publicly in a newspaper, on radio or television, etc.: to advertise a reward.
> 3. to call attention to, in a boastful or ostentatious matter.

Perhaps that's why we've grown to resent advertising and the way it interrupts us—it's not because we are more intolerant than past generations, but because there are increasing demands for our attention and we have more options than ever before. We don't simply have a choice of a handful of radio stations. We can listen to free podcasts that entertain and inform us for hours without trying to get us to buy dog food or double glazing. When was the last time you bought something from the cold-caller who rang just as you were stir-frying vegetables at 6 p.m.? How does it make you feel when a popup appears on a website's landing page before you have time to read a word?

Probably not how you want your customers to feel.

We still think it's okay to interrupt people without any context, for one reason only: because we can.

That was never a good way to make people care. If we want to survive in a world with unlimited choices, we've got no option but to work harder to make sure that *the right people care more.*

I once had a client who came to me having spent $6,000 on an advert in a glossy magazine. She knew the magazine's circulation numbers, but she didn't know if her message had really reached anyone. The phone didn't ring once afterwards. I think she chose to advertise because it felt safe—because if you're in business, that's what you do to get customers and survive. Maybe that's why the worst kind of advertising still exists: because business owners are scared that the phones won't ring tomorrow.

I'm sure the dancing billboard sold a few more pizzas that evening, but we didn't miss not seeing him on the side of the road the next day. And we care about his pizzas (or those of the three other takeaways within a 5km radius) only when we can buy two for the price of one.

WHY YOUR BRAND DOESN'T NEED A UNIQUE SELLING PROPOSITION

In the '90s, Pampers' 'unique selling proposition' (USP) was its claim to be the driest nappy on the market. Procter & Gamble prided itself on this benefit, investing heavily in research and development to maintain that USP. In the end, though, that singular focus blinkered the company's understanding about what mothers really wanted. And while they believed that Pampers was the driest nappy, that wasn't enough to stop mums from buying more of the newer Huggies brand, which appealed to their hearts, not just their heads.

The marketing concept of the unique selling proposition was introduced in the 1940s by the pioneer of television advertising, Rosser Reeves. Reeves invented the term USP to explain how successful advertising (not necessarily great products and services) could convince the masses to switch brands. The golden rule was that adverts must include a USP that essentially said, 'Buy this product, and you will get this specific benefit'. Back then, everyone knew that if you shaved with a Gillette razor, you would 'Look sharp, feel sharp', and that Guinness was 'Good for you'. More than sixty years later, we're trying to make something that applied to an analogue world fit into our digital landscape.

Marketing departments try to pass off cheaper, faster, stronger and longer lasting as unique benefits of a product or service. But when most things are good enough, it gets harder and harder to turn being different into an advantage. Unique by definition means one-of-a-kind, unlike anything else. That was an easy claim to make half a century ago, when there were three kinds of washing powder—not so easy today.

People don't want to be sold on the reasons you think your brand is better or best. They don't want something different. They want something that creates a *difference*.

Starbucks, Google, Instagram, Amazon, Innocent Juices, Oprah, Spanx, and on and on, didn't succeed just because they were different and could tell us how. What makes a brand unique now is the difference it creates—how it affects people's lives and becomes part of their story. When you are organised to create difference, not just to be different, the result is much harder to replicate.

THE SECRET OF DISRUPTIVE INNOVATIONS

People tell us who they are, but we ignore it because we
want them to be who we want them to be.
—DONALD DRAPER, 'THE SUMMER MAN,'
MAD MEN, SEASON 4

When the eyewear retailer Warby Parker began selling boutique-quality glasses at a $95-a-pair price point, they weren't just trying to undercut the bigger players in the industry. But they did that and more, growing the company by 500 percent in just a year and mostly by word of mouth.

Warby Parker set out to change how it felt to buy and wear glasses. The average customer who needs glasses buys a pair every 2.1 years. Warby Parker wanted to make glasses something that people would consider buying in multiples as a way to express themselves, much like women buy shoes and handbags. The founders wanted their customers to think of glasses as accessories they could change to match occasions or moods. Price, quality and their 'buy a pair, give a pair' model enable the company to tell a different story than other retailers, but what changes everything is the story the customer now tells himself about how many pairs of glasses he can own and how often he should buy new ones. Many of Warby Parker's customers buy several pairs of glasses at a time and not just when their prescriptions expire.

Airbnb made people long to experience a destination like a local without the $8 price tag for nuts from the mini-bar. Apple changed how we feel about buying a whole album that probably included songs we didn't care about. Amazon's Kindle made us think of airport bookstores as reference libraries where we browse, but don't buy.

The secret of disruptive innovations and business models isn't that they disrupt an industry; it's that they disrupt people. They change how people feel about something, in a way that's enough to change how they behave. It's entirely possible to look to the future and think about how your customers might be changed tomorrow as a result of what you do today.

While industries work on the assumption that the larvae of today will just be bigger caterpillars tomorrow, the disruptor imagines butterflies.

THE ELEPHANT IN THE MARKETING ROOM

Although many of us may think of ourselves as thinking creatures that feel, biologically we are feeling creatures that think.
—JILL BOLTE TAYLOR,
MY STROKE OF INSIGHT: A BRAIN SCIENTIST'S PERSONAL JOURNEY

I was raised in Dublin, the storytelling capital of the world. There is no place on earth that is more hardwired for story than Ireland, home of Guinness and oversize teapots.

Wikipedia will tell you that the Irish are some of the biggest consumers of tea (and Guinness). What Wikipedia won't tell you is that in Ireland, tea (like Guinness) isn't just a drink—it's a lubricator of story. Small wonder, then, that Irish people are known, as they say themselves, for having 'the gift of the gab'. Sometimes we don't even need the tea (or Guinness) to fuel the stories; we just need an excuse to get together.

When I was five or six and there was nothing to do on a sleepy Sunday afternoon, my dad would drive my little brother and me down to Hector Grey's Sunday market on his Honda 50. One of us would ride on the front, the other on the back—which I'm guessing wasn't strictly legal.

Hector Grey was a silver-haired, silver-tongued shop owner. Watching him was the closest I'd come to witnessing theatre. His stage was a small platform that he erected outside The Woollen Mills, and he beckoned people to come closer—ostensibly so they could hear, but actually, I suspect, so they could feel the heightened emotion and sense of expectation in each other. Hector sold imported hardware and trinkets. He never once described what a product would *do;* he painted a picture of what it would feel like to *have.*

Nobody knew what might be in the boxes on any given Sunday, or how many were in stock. Hector told stories about gold-plated tea sets shipped from exotic Hong Kong, and of Mandarin-scented soaps from Taiwan, places most people in Dublin would never see, even on a map. He framed the scarcity of everything he sold. There was always limited stock and there wasn't much of an opportunity to see the products up close. When Hector finally finished by tapping on the box like a magician about to produce a rabbit from a hat, he explained the bargain he was prepared to give to the first hands that inevitably shot up.

Many of the things we bought on those Sundays were used once, or became a memory at the back of some glass cabinet or at the bottom of the kitchen drawer.

Some might say that Hector was what they would call in Dublin 'a gangster' and that we were idiots for falling for his spiel, when in fact we were all characters playing a part in the same story. We wanted to be taken on a journey. Hector took us there. He didn't try to convince us; he changed how we felt. And like people waiting in line outside the Apple store on iPhone launch day, we weren't there for the box we would take home that afternoon; we were there for the story.

So if people buy the story—if they buy the fortune, not the cookie; the experience, not just the raw ingredients—why don't we as marketers work harder to give people a story to believe in?

Whether we are marketers, consumers, or both, it can be uncomfortable to realise that we are less rational than we think. Harvard Business School professor Gerald Zaltman says that 95 percent of our decision-making takes place in the subconscious mind. This statistic disturbs us on several levels—we like to think we make rational decisions. But as consumers, should we feel like fools because we pay for story and context if those things are what really matter to us? Should Howard Schultz feel bad because he recognised the opportunity in selling coffee by the cup, rather than just beans by the pound, as Starbucks used to do in the old days? Is it wrong to give people what they want wrapped in a story, if the value of what they want is subjective and intangible?

The genius of Hector Grey, Steve Jobs and Howard Schultz lay in two things. These men knew that we were there for the story we couldn't articulate, AND they were not afraid to sell it to us. Perhaps it's time to get comfortable with the fact that if we want to change the world, we need to stop being afraid to tell better true stories. Maybe the time has come to stop trying to convince people and to invest time instead in showing them what we stand for, so that they can choose the stories and brands they want to believe in. Marketing is not a department, it's the story of how we create difference for our customers.

Our Bell Curve Is Melting

LEARNING HOW TO SEE

Peter Drucker famously remarked, 'The most important thing in communication is hearing what isn't said'. Members of a committee might be able to tell you what they think is working or what's broken, but they can't tell you how to matter. And no corporate committee ever in the history of the universe knew what the world was waiting for.

Focus groups can give you an opinion, but they can't tell you how to make meaning from it. You don't find the truth by simply asking for answers. You uncover it by understanding the right questions to ask, by listening and by learning how to really see your customers. The businesses that succeed tell a better story because they have learned to recognise what's true for their customers and then created solutions that match the worldviews, behaviours, habits and rituals those customers live out every day.

Slava Menn and Tivan Amour—self-described 'MIT bike geeks'—are the co-founders of Fortified Bicycle Alliance. Before creating their products and launching their successful Kickstarter campaign, they spoke to hundreds of potential customers and asked them what they loved and hated about biking. The founders 'followed them on rainy night-time commutes, watching them lock their bikes and remove their bike lights.'

They learned that people often forgot their bike lights and, when they did remember them, didn't want the hassle of taking the lights off every time they parked their bikes, so the Fortified Bicycle Alliance team created a light that would lock to handlebars and seat posts. Their potential customers helped them to understand that they needed to build a light that was theft-proof and indestructible, one that would last a lifetime, not just a season. Menn and Tivan didn't just ask people what the problem was; they did everything they could to understand the pain their potential customers experienced. Going to the trouble of understanding how potential customers used their bikes every day enabled Fortified Bicycle Alliance to create a product that people wanted and to raise over $177,000 on Kickstarter. That's a lot of pre-sold bike lights!

The same opportunity to find out the truth is open to you.

TINY MARKETS OF SOMEONE

Mr Ryan owned a corner shop in the small Dublin suburb where I grew up. For over twenty years, the shop supported his family and employed his children while they studied. He didn't seem to worry when yet another big supermarket opened close by. Sure, he knew some of his customers would go there for special offers, but he also knew that he wasn't after the 'market of everyone'. He didn't need everyone to keep coming to his store; he just needed to matter to enough people by doing things the big guys couldn't do, like creating a sense of community and belonging in his little shop. While the big guys chased volume and margins, Mr Ryan sought to understand and build deeper connections and lasting relationships with his customers. He was never too busy to chat about who was coming to visit from England that summer, or to hear about why Mrs Byrne needed an extra soft roll and her husband's favourite Galtee cheese to take to him up at St James' Hospital, because he couldn't stand the food there.

When industry and innovation became very focused on the metric of more, we lost sight of the fact that more wasn't always the best place to start. And then, ironically, the Internet, which could help us to reach everyone, made us realise that there were 'tiny markets of someone'. And as Seth Godin says, the bell curve has melted. Not only is there no longer a mass market, but most of the successful companies, game-changing innovations, and products and services we care about were designed to cater to people at the edges of that curve, not to the average Joe in the middle of it.

How did a tiny yogurt company compete with industry giants who had twenty times their budget and controlled two-thirds of the market? In five years, Chobani went from having almost no revenue to selling a predicted $1 billion worth of yogurt in 2013. They started at the edges, doing things the bigger brands were not prepared to do, like making an authentic Greek yogurt without thickeners, using 'a centuries-old technique of straining to remove excess liquid' for people who wanted to experience difference. Chobani founder Hamdi Ulukaya set out to change what people understood yogurt to be and to shake up the yogurt industry. He wanted to 'make delicious and nutritious Greek Yogurt accessible to everyone'. Ulukaya didn't simply make yogurt using a different technique and superior ingredients; he spent eighteen months putting his heart into creating the perfect cup of yogurt and into building a company that was people-centred rather than profit-centred.

Airbnb went from appealing to people at the edges (who would want to share a stranger's apartment instead of visiting a hotel?) to having over 300,000 listings worldwide in 33,000 cities and booking 10 million nights in 192 countries within five years.

Method entered the household cleaner market, which was dominated by big players like P&G, and differentiated at the edges on results, safety, sustainability, design and scent. The company achieved over 500 percent growth in just three years.

Can you name any brand that's gained traction, loyalty and love during the past decade that didn't begin at the edges? Red Bull, Facebook, Zipcar, TED, Trey Ratcliff, Kickstarter, Instagram, Spanx, Hiut

Denim, Zappos, Kindle, Innocent, PayPal, TaskRabbit and By The Way Bakery. Even Amazon and Apple didn't begin by targeting the market of everyone.

The truth is that the masses don't want to feel like 'the masses'. They want to discern. To choose. To be seen. To matter. Your customers don't want to be just anyone, they want to be someone.

The great brands of the future will be built by those who have worked hard to gain the insight that enables them to whisper 'we see you' to their customers.

Shouting 'notice us' just doesn't cut it anymore.

BUILDING YOUR BRAND ONE PERSON AT A TIME

Growing up in the '70s and '80s meant that I had plenty of opportunities to witness word-of-mouth marketing at close quarters. While the Internet has given us many more ways to spread ideas and the opportunity to use all kinds of tools and tactics, the principles of how people fall in love with ideas hasn't changed for centuries.

The truth is that people don't fall in love with ideas at all. They fall in love with how those ideas, products, services and places make them feel.

The popularity of the hit 3D puzzle of the '70s, the Rubik's Cube, is a classic example of word-of-mouth marketing in action. One minute you'd never heard of the thing. The next, every single kid in the playground had one (or wanted one). Even in schools where it wasn't cool to be smart, kids proudly carried those colourful cubes around, showing how smart they were. They brought their Rubik's Cubes wherever they went and wore the number of sides they could solve like a badge of honour. If you could solve the cube, you were a genius. If you owned one, you were one degree of separation from genius. The Rubik's Cube made being smart cool overnight. Cube owners weren't just playing with a toy or solving a puzzle; they were belonging.

Without any way to share it, apart from one person simply telling another, the Rubik's Cube became the best-selling puzzle toy of all time, not because it was the best puzzle (so few people could actually solve it), but because it was the puzzle with the best story.

We sometimes get lost in the tactics of how to spread the word about our businesses. The old advertising model trapped us for several decades with the notion that if we throw money at it and tell people what to believe, they will buy it. It turns out, though, that getting people to 'BUY IT NOW' is far less important than helping them to believe in your product and service for a lifetime. The most valuable companies in the world, like Apple and Google, don't just create consumers of their products; they create difference and a sense of ownership of the brand.

The companies that have succeeded wildly in the last decade didn't get there with Super Bowl ads; they did it one person at a time. Just like the Rubik's Cube.

PEOPLE DON'T BUY FEATURES; THEY BUY PROMISES

Every day another product, tool, or app comes to market. One more shortcut to something.

Want to save lists, share things, buy, sell, store, capture, talk, listen, watch, wake up, or waste time? There's definitely a feature-filled app that can help you do that.

As marketers we often get bogged down in the features and benefits of what it is we have to offer. We get stuck at the 'telling people what it does' part.

But here's the thing: deep down most people don't care about what the features enable them to do. Why not?

Because people don't want to *do;* they want to *be.* They want to be less busy and more productive, less alone and more connected, less fearful and more safe.

People don't buy features—they buy promises.

INTANGIBLES HAVE A REAL-WORLD VALUE

Once upon a time, earphones were 'functional black', until Apple changed everything by adding a layer of meaning to what was once a commodity worth nothing more than a few dollars. By making earphones 'accessory white', Apple gave iPod owners a way to be noticed and to belong.

The most famous roofline in the world brings a billion dollars a year into the Australian economy. Those vaulted shells don't make Sydney Opera House more functional, but they change how people feel when they stand in front of it. They deliver joy far beyond the cost of the concrete, wood and tiles used to build them. The shells enable us to attach meaning and significance to a building, and they give us a story to tell.

In the real world, a disproportionate amount of value is placed on the tangible. Things we can easily explain, or put our finger on. Of course it's easier to place a value on what can be weighed and measured. And yet all around us, every day we are surrounded by proof that 'soft innovations'— relatively inexpensive, sometimes intangible, but well-considered enhancements of an experience like a package design or outstanding customer service; things that change how people feel about a product or service, and create emotional points of difference—have a real-world value.

Time and again the market proves that the value of stuff is finite, but the meaning we attach to stuff—the experiences we create around it and the stories we tell ourselves about it—has exponential value. The fortune, not the cookie, is what people really care about.

VALUE AND THE MACARON EFFECT

Let's face it, a macaron isn't even a bite. It's gone before you know it, and although your brain knows you've had one, your stomach could beg to differ. Macarons have been around for centuries, but I don't remember seeing the dainty, coloured, every-flavoured sandwiched confections that are now ubiquitous even a few years ago. And they're expensive for what they are in any language or currency, whether it's $3 or €3.

A lot of people don't 'get' macarons (or macaroons, for that matter—and yes, they're different).

> *This is the single most overpriced thing in the history of capitalism. It's a single, stupid little macaroon.*
> —RORY SUTHERLAND ON TWITTER

Macarons are not designed for Rory; they are marketed to a sensibility and, dare I say it, to women. Their value is highly subjective. The thing about a macaron is that much of its value is perceived. The real value is psychological and therefore intangible. It's a sweet treat with damage limitation built in.

A macaron is mostly almonds and egg white, low in fat, gluten free (two things we've come to care about), and so tiny the sugar can hardly count... right? When you're rationalising about how many minutes it's going to take on the treadmill to work it off, a macaron feels like a bargain compared to the other choices in the cake cabinet.

One man's rip-off is another woman's indulgence.

Like most things we buy, or things we value when we have everything we need, macarons are not a product. They are a story we tell ourselves.

THINKING BEYOND CUSTOMER NEEDS

The couple at the café order two teas and one cake with two forks. The story the woman has told herself is that they are sharing the cake she ordered. Halving the damage. The guy quietly sips his tea as she slices the cake into squares and begins eating the smaller pieces, picking around the edges of the rest until she's eaten the lot. The café owner might be happy, of course, because he's made a profit by catering to a need. But I don't think the customer got what she really wanted, which was a tiny cake. No willpower required!

Nobody *needs* a £130.00 pair of jeans made from organic cotton. But there are people who are happy to pay that and then to wait several weeks for their jeans to be handcrafted by Hiut Denim's Grand Master jeans makers in Wales.

And the 40 percent of customers who bought McDonald's milkshakes for breakfast weren't just satisfying their unexpressed needs. They were fulfilling an unspoken desire for a one-handed snack that made their commute less boring and tided them over until lunchtime.

What your customer *does*, not what she thinks or what she *says* she does, leaves clues about what she really wants from you. Maybe the real truth is that people know what they want, but they're just not very good at articulating it.

Truly great brands don't create products and services just to fulfil customer needs. They create for wants, desires, beliefs, behaviours and unexpressed worldviews. The same opportunity is open to you.

EMOTIONAL POINTS OF DIFFERENCE

Singapore's Changi Airport doesn't have the most runways (in fact, it has only two), but it does have a nature trail, complete with sunflowers and butterflies. It's also known as one of the best airports in the world.

The little By The Way Bakery in Hastings-on-Hudson has a rolling pin for a door handle. Even before you set foot inside, you've been given a clue about the intention of the owner and what to expect. You know that the owner cares about the experience customers will have even before they open the door.

Packaging of household cleaners was traditionally clinical. Method made it beautiful. Coffee was once a $1 commodity; Starbucks made it a $4 experience.

When you go the extra mile, people will know, and that knowing changes everything about how they feel about what you do.

Emotional points of difference, the things that are less obvious and sometimes not even articulated, matter. They show people that you care. They mark out brands that stand for something, shape cultures and create followings of loyal customers and brand advocates that no amount of advertising can buy.

WHAT YOU MEASURE MATTERS, BUT WHAT'S HARD TO MEASURE MIGHT MATTER MORE

When return on investment is measured by delight instead of sales or conversions, there's a lot more freedom to be creative, to be bold, or maybe even to be creative and bold.
—Lain Shakespeare, Nonprofit Brand Manager at MailChimp

It's easy to count Facebook likes and numbers of Twitter followers. And we've found ways to justify the return on investment of a billboard that's passed by 20,000 people every day. It's easy to advocate for doing things that we can measure. A metric of any kind feels safe, *and* it's got deniability built in.

But what's the ROI of a Google Doodle?

The significance of a paragraph of engaging copy on a garment-care label that makes your customer laugh?

The value of the joy experienced by a customer when a complaint is well handled?

The impact of empathy offered at the right moment?

Impact, connection, loyalty and love can't easily be measured, which is why business hasn't traditionally made these things a priority. Perhaps it's time that changed.

The things we can't measure might be far more valuable to our businesses than the things we can.

RELEVANCE IS THE NEW REMARKABLE

Our interruption tolerance threshold is decreasing at a rapid rate and businesses and advertisers know it. In Australia we even have a Do Not Knock sticker that people can display close to their doors to keep unwanted salespeople from interrupting them at home. Are people demanding one where you live?

The people you want to reach decide what's relevant to them. Of course it's been obvious for a long time that the Internet, remote controls and mobile devices have caused an attention shift. But what's happening now goes beyond finding new and different ways to capture attention. People will no longer stand for being interrupted. It's no good saying 'print more fliers' or 'put out another ad campaign', because you might as well be whistling into the wind without meaning or context.

There is no shortcut to creating things that people care for and want to talk about, or to building customer relationships that endure. No easy way to reach everyone. But there are better and more rewarding ways to engage with the people who want to hear from you, like creating helpful content on your blog or treating your most loyal customers differently so that they feel valued.

Don't just work out how to wave your arms at the masses. Build something just for the people who matter. Relevance is the new remarkable.

WHAT DO YOUR CUSTOMERS WANT?

Let's look at some cold, hard and fun facts.

A search for *#me* on Instagram one morning in mid-September gave me over 123 million results. Just eighteen hours later, a further 466,000 had been added. Let's round that up to half a million a day, which means that 26,000 photos with the hashtag *#me* are uploaded to Instagram every hour of every day. As I'm writing a couple of months later, the total is almost 166 million. I wonder what it will be by the time you read this.

It's impossible now to create or sell anything without considering what your potential customers believe or understanding what they care about. And increasingly what they care about is what the choices they make, and the things they consume, buy, share, or relate to, say about them.

Yes, there are a heck of a lot of people who care that the chicken in their curry was happy before it died. And as clothing retailer Patagonia understands, to the benefit of their bottom line, not everyone wants throwaway fashion. Some people are willing to pay a premium for products that are made to last and don't harm the environment unnecessarily.

People are telling us what they care about and it isn't our products. It's *their* journey, *their* story, the meaning they want to create in *their* lives.

It turns out that the key to creating difference is to make something that changes how people feel and makes them fall just a little more in love, not with what we sell but with themselves.

Made To Matter

RETHINKING GROUPTHINK

I once had a conversation with a passionate *Fortune* 500 company executive. He and his team were desperately trying to find more ways to make their product and story matter to customers. Focus groups weren't helping them to get to the heart of the story they needed to tell.

Here's what I shared with him; maybe it's something for you to consider, too. Firstly, focus groups probably won't get you to where you want to go, because their job is to find a way to articulate something they feel. They are paid to give you logical explanations—'Why did you prefer the red packaging?' 'It stood out on the shelf; it was bright and reminded me of fresh ingredients'—when understanding and empathy are what's required. Focus groups might help you to build something that looks more perfect to the group, but groupthink doesn't help you to create things that were made to matter.

We assume that the most valuable data is static and lives on graphs and in spreadsheets. But turning to the graphs first, last and always to get to know your customers is like looking at a child's development purely on a growth chart. You're definitely not getting the whole picture. While we've been busy analysing the data for information, we've forgotten that what we wanted all along was the insight.

The truth of what we need to know and some of the most valuable data live in plain sight. The wrinkled nose of the diner. The sigh of the shopper waiting in line. The posture of the customer as she walks out the door. What she packed in her bag before she left home this morning. How she goes about her day. Noticing what people *do* is often more valuable to us than listening to what they *say* they think.

Secondly, stop advertising, or at least be honest about why you're doing it. If you're advertising to make your franchisees feel safe, then fine, but you might find it's better to educate them about more effective ways to market by baking marketing into your products and services, not by paying to sprinkle it on at the end. Advertising might help you to make *things* sound better, but what people really want from you is to make *life* better. You have to work out how you're going to do that before you think about how to sell a single thing.

THE P THAT MARKETING FORGOT

So, if we wanted to sell anything in the last half-century, the four Ps of the Marketing Mix were there to guide us. It was pretty straightforward, really. Decide what you want to sell at what price, tell prospects what they should think about it, and keep finding more ways to tell them over and over again.

The P that the old Marketing Mix forgot, one that no business can afford to forget nowadays, was people. Where were we, the people who were putting our hands in pockets, our money on the counter, and our loyalty on the line in all of this? It turns out that our wallets were the thing that was part of the mix. We were seen as a homogenous group, prospects, consumers, targets and traffic—anything but human.

We were demographics outside the brand's circle of influence, disconnected from the activities of Monstrous Corp., with no thoughts or feelings required. We were worker bees who transformed into walking wallets at the weekend.

Today we are powerful influencers who discern and care, and want and choose.

Because we can.

DEMOGRAPHICS VS. WORLDVIEWS

Our understanding of the values, attitudes and behaviours of the most desirable customers has shifted. According to consumer behaviourist Ross Honeywill, there is a New Economic Order—'a growing class of high-value consumers that is powering the economy and re-imagining society'. The people in this group, referred to as NEOs and contrasted with Traditionals, 'have progressive social and political attitudes,... earn and spend more than anyone else, are digital activists,... are natural leaders and control freaks, and actively redefine their world and the rules of engagement for businesses that inhabit their world'. The majority of this group are in the top third of discretionary spenders.

Why is it helpful to understand the worldview of this particular group of people? As Honeywill says in *One Hundred Thirteen Million Markets of One*, '... consumer behaviour is largely predictable once you understand that it is not demographics, income or any other single factor that drives spending, but a combination of distinct values, attitudes and behaviours held by the two main groups in society'. In other words, relying on demographic profiles just doesn't cut it anymore; you have to dig deeper.

It's improbable now to expect that you can presume everything about your customers just because you know their age, sex and postcode. In a digital world that enables ever increasing possibilities and choices, people are no longer constrained by location, age or gender, and they are not so easy to put into a box, either.

It's far more helpful to think holistically about the people you want to serve. In addition to considering their problems or needs, you need to understand what they value and how they think and feel. Are your customers driven by their love of great design, or do they simply care that the product works? Do they value convenience over comfort?

Perhaps they are more concerned with their impact on the planet than the price they pay for something.

The businesses that succeed tomorrow will be the ones that invest time today to work out how to bring products and service to market that show they understand the wants, needs and unexpressed desires of their customers.

WHAT'S THE STORY?

For the thirty-one years he was alive, my little brother never greeted me by saying 'hello' or 'how are you?' The only question Johnny ever asked was, 'what's the story?'

This is a common way to greet people in Ireland. It stands for lots of things. Hello, what's up?, what's going on?, how are you? I believe the English expression stems from the Irish *aon scéal, which literally means 'any story?' or 'have you any story?'*

I love that. It's such an open-ended question, unlike any other greeting you could express. 'Hello' stops the conversation dead. 'How are you?' can simply require a one-word answer. But 'what's the story?' means 'tell me everything that's important to you right now'. And the world is so, so ready for more of this. People are very tired of being ignored, of being the 99 percent, of being managed, used, exploited, homogenised, tricked, controlled and forgotten. They want to be a part of something, to have a story to tell, to have something to believe in. They want—actually, no, they expect—the people they do business with to understand them and to build around their wants, their needs and even their unexpressed desires. And it's our job, yours and mine, to give them that. It's time to stop thinking about how we can take the money first. It's time to really understand the answer to the question 'what's the story?'

EVERYONE OWNS THE TRUTH

As soon as my long-haul flight from Dubai landed (two hours behind schedule), people began wrestling bags and jostling on the spot, eager to get off the plane. The priority of course was people with connecting flights who might have a chance of making them. For others it was too late and they'd be spending the night at the airport hotel.

A woman began to push forward from two rows behind. 'I need to get off', she said. Apparently her daughter and baby granddaughter were waiting.

'Don't we all!' a fellow passenger barked back.

Every single passenger on board had their own version of an emergency, which made it difficult for them to stand in someone else's shoes.

As business owners and marketers (let alone people), that's exactly what we must learn to get better at doing. If we don't want to risk becoming irrelevant to the very people we want to matter to, then we need to understand that everyone has their own version of the truth and we'd better know what their version of the truth is.

THE CURRENCY OF THE FUTURE

In a post-advertising world, almost every businessperson I speak to is wrestling, not with the future of business and storytelling, but with the future of *their* story. How do traditional businesses born in the industrial age, those that thrived in a *Mad Men*-esque world, adapt and find new ways to be seen and heard? How do digital businesses create intimacy, when what they probably want is scale? How does anyone stay relevant in a world where expectations shift daily beneath our feet and fickle people change their behaviour? Businesses know that people are voting with their wallets for companies they want to see succeed and not necessarily for the company with the biggest marketing budget.

The future we seem to be imagining is about tactics, and platforms, and technology that makes us feel somehow more able to connect and less relevant all at once. We picture a paperless and scary place, where print and traditional advertising no longer exist because they have no impact. We worry about a future we are racing to keep pace with just so we can stay in the game, where our messages and stories seem to lose permanence and significance.

And the irony is that the answers we're searching for lie in the past and the present, in looking each other in the eye, and ourselves in the mirror, before we try to pre-empt the future.

Before paper, ink and white space, we had only words. The words and stories we paid attention to had to have meaning for us, or they didn't get passed on. We gathered around campfires to listen, and sat around tables talking and drinking tea, or got comfortable with a book on our mother's lap. The medium didn't matter; what mattered was the connection, the animal warmth and the trust. Now suddenly we feel a bit lost as to how to re-create that at scale in a digital world, so we focus on the tactics instead of the truth.

As our circles of intimacy contract and our circles of influence expand— how many people know their neighbours anymore and yet have 500 'friends' on Facebook?—it gets harder and harder to look people in the eye, to let them know they can trust us. And yet that's what we have to find a way to do, not because our businesses won't survive if we don't, but because *we* won't survive without that connection both to doing work that matters and to each other.

The currency of the future was also the currency of the past; it's simply about intentionally creating deeper connections to each other. Before we imagine a world through Google Glass, or a future of wearables, digital storytelling and connection platforms of every kind, we need to acknowledge the truth about where we came from and why we're here.

The future might not be as unpredictable or complicated as we think.

THE DIFFERENCE MODEL

Every day businesses of all stripes, from *Fortune* 500 companies to lone entrepreneurs working from cafés, use a traditional product development model to conceive, create and sell products and services without knowing as much as they can about whom those products are for and why these people would want those services. The first question on everyone's lips is, 'how do I sell this idea?' It turns out that we're starting in the wrong place, with the wrong question.

The Difference Model flips the product development sequence on its head. Instead of starting with the idea, it begins with an examination of people's current reality and explores what's possible in a world where the problems and desires of those people are solved and met. As I explained earlier, difference happens at the intersection of truth, opportunity and action. You can't build successful businesses, sustain great ideas, or create difference without empathy. Products developed using the old model of the industrial age were built to sell. Ideas developed using the Difference Model are made to matter.

Here's how the co-founders of IDEO, who are responsible for some of the world's greatest innovations, explain the importance of empathy in business innovation in their book *Creative Confidence*.

> The notion of empathy and human-centeredness is still not widely practiced in many corporations. Business people rarely navigate their own websites or watch how people use their products in a real-world setting. And if you do a word association with "business person," the word "empathy" doesn't come up much.

What do we mean by empathy in terms of creativity and innovation? For us, it's the ability to see an experience through another person's eyes, to recognize why people do what they do. ... Gaining empathy can take some time and resourcefulness. But there is nothing like observing the person you're creating something for to spark new insights. ...We've found that figuring out what other people actually need is what leads to the most significant innovations. In other words, empathy is a gateway to the better and sometimes surprising insights that can help distinguish your idea or approach.
—DAVID KELLEY AND TOM KELLEY,
CREATIVE CONFIDENCE

Almost half a century after the introduction of the four Ps of the Marketing Mix (remember, product, price, place and promotion), which sold things aimed at the masses, we're not just reimagining the way stories about our businesses, ideas, products and services are told. We're creating a new framework for understanding what people want, recognising opportunities, bringing ideas to market and doing business, and this framework enables us to create things that need to exist in the world. I call this framework the Difference Model. It's designed to be the foundation for building any business idea. The Difference Model is built around six pillars: principles, purpose, people, personal, perception and product.

The Difference Model

PRINCIPLES

> *If you want to make something new, start with*
> *understanding. Understanding what's already present,*
> *and understanding the opportunities in what's not.*
> *Most of all, understanding how it all fits together.*
> —SETH GODIN

What's the truth about us, the industry, the market and the people we want to serve?

Principles are fundamental truths, cornerstones and guiding lights. Every organisation, business venture or tiny project is founded on them; sometimes they haven't been explored or articulated, but they still exist. When we set out to start something, we have an understanding of the what, the where and the why of it. We might know that we have resources and limitations, parameters that we've got to work within. We may not label them truths, but that's what they are, and as we strive to create the story that will resonate with the people we want to serve, it's important to consider them.

Principles can be divided into three categories: the truth about you, the truth about the industry or the market, and the truth about the people you want to matter to.

The truth about you: Firstly, there is the truth about you, your people, or your organisation and what you stand for. What do the people who are building this business believe and believe in? (Your organisation might consist of just you, which is totally fine.) What are your goals? What's the big dream? Your assets and liabilities? Your strengths and weaknesses? Those truths influence the story you can tell your customers. Steve Jobs and Steve Wozniak each had different strengths, which they played to when they founded Apple. One of the Steves was a creative big-picture person; the other one was into the details. The founders of Airbnb had little in the way of hard cash to build their business at first, but what they did have was a creative vision for what could be and the design chops and tech skills to execute it. Understanding the whole truth about you means that you can play to your strengths and have a strategy to overcome weaknesses.

The truth about the industry or the market: What is the truth about the state of the industry that you work in, or the one you hope to enter or change? The iPhone was developed around a truth that cell phones were purely functional. Steve Jobs wanted his engineers to create the first phone that people would fall in love with. As former Apple product manager Bob Brochers explains, 'The idea was, he wanted to create something that was so instrumental and integrated in peoples' lives that you'd rather leave your wallet at home than your iPhone'. Dollar Shave Club was founded on the premise that men were sick of paying for shave tech they didn't need.

The founders of MOO.com knew back in 2004 that printing was still big business. They discovered that online printing companies were leveraging cheaper technology to reduce printing costs, but they also understood that many Web-based printing companies sacrificed quality for price. MOO knew that there were people who would appreciate great, cost-effective design. So they set out to disrupt a very traditional $100 billion industry by marrying what they knew people cared about with the convenience of an online marketplace and outstanding customer service. The truth about the industry could be the cornerstone of your story because it speaks to the problem you want to solve and the need you want to meet.

The truth about the people you want to matter to: What's the truth about the reality your prospective customers are living with? What do they believe? How do those beliefs influence how they behave today, and how might they change what they do tomorrow? What problems do they want you to solve? What might they need? What are their unexpressed desires? There is nothing more important to any business today than understanding the worldview of its customers and the reality they live with. Products, services and ideas that fly are created by understanding how to solve real-world problems. Spanx founder Sara Blakely became the youngest self-made female billionaire by understanding the reality millions of women lived with every day when they pulled on their clothes. Sara designed body-shaping underwear that solved the problem of visible panty lines, because she experienced (and solved) the problem firsthand. She knew that women wanted to look as good as they could in their clothes.

PURPOSE

> *The fifty top performing brands, in good economic times and in bad, were the ones that were founded on what Jim Stengel calls an ideal. In other words, they had a bigger purpose, a mission that the company set out to fulfill. For example, Google exists to satisfy the curiosity of anyone with access to the Internet; Method, the household cleaning brand, wants to inspire happy, healthy homes.*
> —Bernadette Jiwa,
> *The Fortune Cookie Principle*

Why do we exist?

Why does your business exist? Your purpose is not what you do, but why you do it. Bringing a product to market isn't enough. You need to consider *Why this product? Why now?* And think about the bigger impact you want to create in the world. When Jane Ní Dhulchaointigh invented Sugru—a brand of silicone rubber that can be used to fix, hack and reinvent things—she was very clear about what the impact of the product could be. Jane wanted to build a culture that empowered people to fix things, adapt things and make them more functional and longer lasting, rather than to replace or be frustrated by them.

PEOPLE

> *But increasingly companies around the globe are
> looking to inform design with greater insight into the
> makings of their uses, not just their products, and what
> drives use in the first place.*
> —JAN CHIPCHASE,
> *HIDDEN IN PLAIN SIGHT*

Who is this for exactly?

Who are the people you want to serve? What do they value? What do they care about? What's their current reality? Don't think simply in terms of demographics; think about your customers' worldview and how they navigate the world from day to day.

Crafting your intention around the difference your product or service will create in the lives and stories of these people, your customers, is what will enable you to go beyond simply being another alternative in a crowded marketplace.

Dollar Shave Club understood that men really resent paying too much for celebrity-endorsed, feature-filled, quadruple-blade, titanium razors and that they were overwhelmed by the choices. The founders of Dollar Shave Club also figured out that men often shaved with dull blades because they had forgotten to pick up new razors.

PERSONAL

> *We see our customers as invited guests to a party, and we are the hosts. It's our job every day to make every important aspect of the customer experience a little bit better.*
> —JEFF BEZOS, FOUNDER AND CEO, AMAZON.COM

How can we change how people feel?

How can you become more relevant and significant to the people you want to serve? How can your business be about making them live as a better version of themselves? What difference does your product make to them?

How you make your customers feel about themselves in the presence of your brand is what matters. With their One for One model, TOMS made customers feel good about buying footwear. For every pair of shoes they sell, the company donates a pair to a child in the developing world. So every time a TOMS customer puts on her shoes, she remembers that she has also provided a pair for a child who had nothing to wear on her feet.

PERCEPTION

> *Our personal beliefs define our choices, shape our lives and, collectively, determine our futures. Nothing is more important than belief.*
> —Tom Asacker

What do people believe? What would we like them to believe about us and about themselves in the presence of our product?

What your customers believe about you far outweighs anything you tell them to think. We connect to each other around our beliefs. Our beliefs also help us to connect more deeply with ourselves. Our beliefs drive our behaviour. Our beliefs and behaviours are the foundation of cultures. The most successful brands and businesses shape and enhance our cultures. Successful businesses are built on being believed and believed in, not just noticed.

What do your customers believe about you?

What would you like them to believe and say about your brand?

What would you have to do to get them to do and say that?

What do they want to believe about themselves?

So many of the great businesses which have thrived in the last five years were founded, and/or have thrived, in competitive markets because they understood the beliefs of the people they wanted to serve.

The Little Veggie Patch Co. in Melbourne helps people to grow their own food, even if they have only a tiny space. The company's Veggie Crates enable people to install their own edible gardens; the Little Veggie Patch Co. edible garden workshops sell out; and the company's seeds, books and other educational and fun products keep people on track. The founders, who were backyard farmers and bloggers, decided to build their business by serving the growing number of young people, women and real food enthusiasts who care about provenance and about taking responsibility for what they eat. The company created products for those people.

PRODUCT

Make something people want.
—PAUL GRAHAM

What do people *really* want? What value does your product or service create for customers?

What product or service matches the worldview, needs and unexpressed desires of the people you want to serve? What will it take to make them fall in love with your product or service?

Don't just seek to find holes in the market or to gain mind share. Set out to fill a void in people's lives.

When you have all of the pieces of the puzzle in place, you'll be ready to bring that product to the people who actually wanted it in the first place.

The founders of the Uber app, which connects passengers with available drivers without the need to stand out in the rain to hail a cab, understood that people were often frustrated by the unpredictability and logistics of using cabs. The co-founders knew that the people they wanted to reach out to with their service—people who 'just wanted to push a button and get a ride'—valued their time and would pay for convenience. With the Uber app, users can book a driver, see how long it will take for the car to arrive, track the driver's journey to them, pay for the ride without using cash, and get the receipt—all via their smartphone.

USING THE DIFFERENCE MAP: CASE STUDIES

What follows are ten business case studies that were created using the Difference Model. Each one is plotted on the Difference Map so that you can see how it works in practice. The businesses profiled are ones that I believe are creating difference for their customers. I had input from some of the founders, but mostly these are my interpretations based on my research and knowledge of the companies. These case studies are designed to illustrate how to use the Difference Map; they are not actual business plans supplied by the companies discussed, although I am very grateful to them for giving me a story to tell by doing the work they do.

For more on these case studies and to see others created using the Difference Model and the Difference Map, visit www.difference.is on the Web.

Download your free copy of the Difference Map* from www.difference. is. Print multiples, enlarge them, stick Post-it notes on them, draw on them, scribble on them and share them with your team.

*The Difference Map is under copyright. Under copyright law and in the interests of good karma, you can't repurpose, reproduce, publish or adapt the Difference Map without the author's consent.

AUSTRALASIAN MEDICAL JOURNAL

The AMJ is an open-access online medical journal that launched in 2007. Focusing on health innovation and debate, the journal serves a global community of emerging and early career researchers. The reality facing many academics (not just in the field of health) is the need to get their research published in order for their careers to progress. Quite rightly, gatekeepers in this industry use a rigorous peer-review process to protect the public from unethical research and spurious claims. However, the established journals own the industry and dominate the conversation. They get many more papers than they can publish, so established researchers have a better chance of having their work published than new researchers do. The AMJ set out to be the place that gave a voice to emerging and early career researchers who were doing great work, but found it hard to get published in traditional journals. The journal not only peer-reviews papers but also gives researchers advice on how they might improve their chances of being published, provides a service for people who need help with English, and waives publication fees for those from developing countries.

See a full-sized, 8.5x11 version of the AMJ case study on www.difference.is

the difference map

CREATED FOR: Australasian Medical Journal

DATE:

PRINCIPLES

Truth about me/us
We're experienced and enthusiastic. We have access to expertise and a deep understanding of the problem.

Truth about the market/industry
Monopoly: traditional medical journals are dominated by a small group of publishers.
Hard to publish in traditional journals.
Long time frames from submission to publication.
Success defined by the medical publishing industry's parameters and worldview.
Journals look for reasons to reject rather than support.

Truth about the people I/we want to serve
Inexperienced researchers.
Find it hard to publish.
Need help with writing and English.
Need to publish for career advancement.

PURPOSE	PEOPLE	PERSONAL	PERCEPTION	PRODUCT
Why do we exist?	Who is this for? What do they care about?	How can we change how people feel? How can we help them live better lives?	What do they believe? What would we like them to believe about us?	What do people really want or need? How do we create value for our customers?
To provide a platform to expose, debate, discuss and promote advances and innovations in health care that wouldn't normally see the light of day.	Early career researchers.	Normally takes months to get rejected or published; we will fix that by standing in the researchers' shoes.	Publishing is hard: the submission process is lengthy and complicated.	Online medical journal with high-quality peer-reviewed articles.
	Those publishing for the first or second time.			
	People who need to publish fast.	Respond quickly.	New researchers fear they will be rejected out of hand.	Free access to articles.
To support emerging researchers with publication and promotion.	Researchers with pilot studies.	Support non-English speakers. Look for reasons to support rather than reject.	AMJ is fast, helpful and responsive.	Affordable publishing for researchers in developing countries.
To raise the profile of emerging researchers.	Those who need more support than traditional journals can offer.	Use pricing that embraces everyone.	AMJ looks for reasons to publish rather than to reject.	Easy online process to publication.
To support the career development of relatively junior people on editorial boards.	Researchers from developing countries.			Guidance (empathetic experts guide academics through the process).
	Researchers who need to publish in a journal which is PubMed indexed.			Open-access journal with PubMed indexation.

55

BY THE WAY BAKERY

By The Way Bakery is a unique, old-fashioned bakery offering gluten-free and dairy-free treats and desserts in New York City. Everything at the bakery is made by hand from scratch in small batches.

See a full-sized, 8.5x11 version of the By The Way Bakery case study on www.difference.is

the difference map

CREATED FOR: By The Way Bakery

DATE:

PRINCIPLES

Truth about me/us

We want to bring joy and make people happy.
Hardwired for pride in what we do.
We want to be an integral part of our village.
Fair. Caring. Stand for what matters.
Not willing to compromise on quality.
Our team is essential to our success. We want to give them the best so they can give their best.

Truth about the market/industry

The market for gluten-free products is experiencing double-digit growth and is expected to exceed $6.2 billion by 2018.
There is a lack of excellence and quality in the market.
Some businesses in the food industry cut corners; there is a culture of taking shortcuts.
The baking industry is becoming a process of assembly rather than a craft to be mastered.

Truth about the people I/we want to serve

Mostly local; some visitors from out of town.
Some—but not all—of our customers need gluten- or dairy-free products.
Don't want to be made to feel different.
Come to enjoy a treat and to feel special.

PURPOSE	PEOPLE	PERSONAL	PERCEPTION	PRODUCT
Why do we exist?	Who is this for? What do they care about?	How can we change how people feel? How can we help them live better lives?	What do they believe? What would we like them to believe about us?	What do people really want or need? How do we create value for our customers?
To delight all who enter the bakery or taste By The Way Bakery products.	Local people; many live in the village.	Exclude nobody. Serve the whole community, not just people with dietary requirements.	Gluten-free products are for people with coeliac disease.	High-quality baked goods, made from scratch with the best ingredients.
To provide sweets of the highest calibre, notwithstanding the constraints on ingredients.	Visitors from out of town need a reason to come.	Develop a relationship with locals.	Gluten-free products are healthier.	Baked goods so delicious that they shatter the perception of what gluten- and dairy-free goods taste like, and people won't think about what's not in the cakes.
To serve both the people who need our products because of allergies and dietary restrictions and the people who will enjoy them because they taste so good.	Those seeking our gluten-free baked goods.	Invest in making people feel like this was made just for them.	Gluten-free is tasteless and unappetizing.	
	Often feel excluded because they can't eat what others eat.	Convey quality in everything we do, from cakes to packaging to remembering our customers' names and favourite products.	Specialist baked goods are always more expensive.	Packaging that feels like a gift.
		Use the best ingredients (French butter, finest flour). Absolutely no compromise on this.	You wouldn't eat gluten-free unless you had no choice.	
		Donate beautiful products to community events.	We want them to think this is the best cookie they have ever tasted.	

57

MOO.COM

MOO is an online printing business founded in 2004. MOO wants to make great design accessible to everyone. The company uses the Internet and new technology to make printing both cost-effective and gorgeous. As they say on their website, MOO set out to 'disrupt the $100 billion global print industry by combining the values of professional design with the accessibility and reach of the web. MOO prints millions of cards a month and has hundreds of thousands of customers in over 180 countries. MOO has also become a much-loved brand, with a 75% NetPromoter rating'.

See a full-sized, 8.5x11 version of the MOO.com case study on www.difference.is

CREATED FOR: MOO.com

DATE:

the difference map

PRINCIPLES

Truth about me/us

Design is key to everything we do. We believe design tells a story about who we are and what we stand for. We love high-quality print. We are a values-led business: we believe in design, innovation, community and excellence. Excited to come to work every day.

Truth about the market/industry

$100 billion industry. Many other printers have chosen to use new technologies and the Internet to simply reduce the costs (and often the quality) of printing. Very traditional. Stale and lacking in innovation. Relying on old business models.

Truth about the people I/we want to serve

Individuals and companies that don't follow the crowd. Creatives and entrepreneurs. Appreciate great design. Need stationery and business cards that make a statement and help them stand out. Want to express their individuality. Need to look professional.

PURPOSE	PEOPLE	PERSONAL	PERCEPTION	PRODUCT
Why do we exist?	**Who is this for? What do they care about?**	**How can we change how people feel? How can we help them live better lives?**	**What do they believe? What would we like them to believe about us?**	**What do people really want or need? How do we create value for our customers?**
To provide great design for everyone'.	Our customers are ambitious, clever, resourceful, passionate and nice.	Encourage active conversations and communication with our customers.	Good design matters.	Quality and attention to detail.
To be the best printer on the Internet.	Care about making a great first impression.	Create better products for our customers by listening to them and understanding their needs.	Design is one of the ways they tell their story.	Innovative, customisable business cards and stationery.
To 'disrupt the $100 billion global print industry by combining the values of professional design with the accessibility and reach of the web'.	Want to change the world, or their corner of it.	Communicate what we stand for in everything we do, from the tone of our website copy to the kind of products we launch.	Design can demonstrate their values and value to the world.	Full-colour products: premium paper.
To change the world one card at a time.	Many run online businesses.	Give our customers something to talk about and share with friends.	We want them to experience us as the best printer in the world.	Short print runs.
	Our customers are entrepreneurial and often work independently or in small teams.	Create products and services that allow customers to connect their online and offline brands		The ability to print a different image on each card, creating a pocket-sized portfolio or catalogue.
				Great user experience on the website for easy card design.
				Packaging and copy that are part of how we add intangible value.

SUGRU

Sugru is 'a self-setting rubber that can be formed by hand'. 'No big deal', I hear you say. But this stuff, which can be moulded like Play-doh, 'bonds to almost anything and turns into a strong, flexible silicone rubber overnight'. Sugru withstands extreme cold, heat and water. All this goes to say that you can use Sugru to improve, adapt, hack, mend, reimagine and redesign products to suit your needs. People have used Sugru to adapt oars, ski poles, and cameras, to make iPhone cable storage, fix broken keys and on and on.

See a full-sized, 8.5x11 version of the Sugru case study on www.difference.is

♠ the difference map

CREATED FOR: Sugru

DATE:

PRINCIPLES

Truth about me/us	Truth about the market/industry	Truth about the people I/we want to serve
Inventors, material scientists, designers, video makers, business and production people. Driven, determined, persistent. Entrepreneurial. Dreamers and visionaries.	We live in a modern throwaway culture of mass manufacture that sacrifices quality for cheapness. So many products are badly designed or not designed to last. Dominated by large multinational corporations selling via retail outlets. Anonymous corporations have big marketing budgets and no direct relationship with customers.	Smart, creative and inventive. Have a can-do attitude. Hackers, fixers and improvers. Problem-solvers who want to take control and sort things out for themselves. Want to share their ideas so that they might help others.

PURPOSE	PEOPLE	PERSONAL	PERCEPTION	PRODUCT
Why do we exist?	**Who is this for? What do they care about?**	**How can we change how people feel? How can we help them live better lives?**	**What do they believe? What would we like them to believe about us?**	**What do people really want or need? How do we create value for our customers?**
To help the world get fixing and customising again.	Care about the world we live in and want to make it better.	Make it easy for people to adapt, improve and modify their stuff so it works better for them.	We've gotten out of the habit of being resourceful and fixing things.	Unique, patented technology with properties that enable it to be versatile and more useful.
To go beyond 'making do'—to take control and repair, modify and evolve the products we own so that they work longer, harder and better for us.	Smart, inventive, creative, resourceful.	Democratise the customisation of anything.	It's just as cheap to replace something as fix it.	Rubber that is soft, strong, and flexible, sticks to anything, air-cures, is waterproof, is stable at high temperatures, and is grippy but also removable.
To provide solutions that are economical, sustainable, and sensible.	Frugal.	Have a direct relationship with our customers. Make their stories part of our story.	We want to help people to get back into the habit of fixing things, making them last longer and work better for them.	The ability to fix things and make them work better.
To grow Sugru into one of the most awesome and meaningful household products in the world.		Sell directly to our customers. Showcase how users hack things with Sugru on our website and through social media channels. Provide a forum where users can ask us questions.		Clever solutions to everyday problems.

WARBY PARKER

Warby Parker is an online eyewear retailer, social commerce company and lifestyle brand. It is now adding retail outlets in response to growth and customer demand.

See a full-sized, 8.5x11 version of the Warby Parker case study on www.difference.is

the difference map

CREATED FOR: Warby Parker

DATE:

PRINCIPLES

Truth about me/us

Passionate about what we do.

Business-school graduates, but no tech expertise on the founding team.

Knowledge of eyewear manufacturing through work in non-profits in the developing world.

Attract and employ talented Millennials who want to do work that matters.

Truth about the market/industry

$65 billion industry.

Oligopoly.

Only 1% of eyewear was sold online before Warby Parker launched.

Illusion of choice. One company owns many brands.

Need to introduce your brand through a trusted source. Industry focused, not customer centric.

Truth about the people I/we want to serve

Want to replace their glasses more than once every two years when their prescriptions expire.

Savvy and fashion conscious; appreciate quality.

Millennials.

Value trust and authenticity.

People in the developing world need access to eyewear that makes them feel good.

PURPOSE	PEOPLE	PERSONAL	PERCEPTION	PRODUCT
Why do we exist?	Who is this for? What do they care about?	How can we change how people feel? How can we help them live better lives?	What do they believe? What would we like them to believe about us?	What do people really want or need? How do we create value for our customers?
To build a global lifestyle brand that has a positive impact on the world.	New Economic Order.	Customer service is everything.	Glasses are expensive.	Quality.
To build a brand that stands for fun, creativity, purpose and beautiful design.	Discerning; they care about style but also about social issues and the environment.	Build trust and community.	There is lots of choice.	Fair price point.
	Don't expect a high level of caring from typical retail brands.	Offer great experience.	You need to go into a store to buy your glasses.	Good value.
	Like to have choices in their eyewear and like to treat eyewear as fashion statements, not just functional objects.	Provide free home try-ons.	They would never consider buying their glasses anywhere else because of the affinity they feel to our brand.	Looking great.
		Engage with customers through social media.		Doing good (WP's one-for-one model donates a pair of glasses for every pair sold).
		Own the customer relationship. Engage with customers where they want to be and shop.		Environmental responsibility (WP is carbon neutral).
		Create content that people want to engage with and share.		Free home try-ons; free shipping and returns.
				Great user experience on the website.

AIRBNB

Airbnb is a community-driven hospitality company. It provides an online marketplace where people can list, discover and rent spaces and unique accommodations around the world.

See a full-sized, 8.5x11 version of the Airbnb case study on www.difference.is

difference

the difference map

CREATED FOR: Airbnb

DATE:

PRINCIPLES

Truth about me/us

Entrepreneurial designers.
Experienced software engineer with a Computer Science degree from Harvard.
Passionate about people.
Love solving real-world problems.
Tenacious.
Creative problem-solvers.

Truth about the market/industry

Travel and tourism industry's total contribution to world GDP is $6.3 trillion.
Travel and tourism sustained 255 million jobs in 2011, and provide 1 in 12 of all jobs in the world.
Travel accommodation in cities is dominated by hotel chains in areas close to city centres.
Hotels don't offer a truly personalized vacation experience.

Truth about the people I/we want to serve

Travelers:
Love travelling and/or meeting new people.
Need a place to stay that won't break the bank.
Want experiences that are out of the ordinary.
Are tired of the sanitised hotel experience.

Hosts:
Need to earn extra money.

PURPOSE	PEOPLE	PERSONAL	PERCEPTION	PRODUCT
Why do we exist?	**Who is this for? What do they care about?**	**How can we change how people feel? How can we help them live better lives?**	**What do they believe? What would we like them to believe about us?**	**What do people really want or need? How do we create value for our customers?**
To change the way people experience the world.	Tired of sameness of travel experiences.	Help real people create personal experiences.	Hotels are expensive and impersonal.	A secure platform where they can list and book a place to stay—almost any kind of space, almost anywhere.
	Enjoy connecting with others. Love to research and plan their trips.	Help people create connections that may last a lifetime.	Service in hotels is not as authentic as it could be.	A way to connect people who need a place to stay with people who have space to rent.
	Travel more than the average person.	Don't use a cookie-cutter formula.	Travellers will never feel like strangers in a strange town again.	A seamless online experience that allows them to discover, enquire about, book and pay for a place to stay.
	Have a sense of adventure.	Help provide the most authentic hosting in the world.		
	Want a more bespoke personalised travel experience.	Help create a growing community of users.		The ability to rate each other and offer feedback, which helps other members of the community.
	Enjoy sharing their experiences with friends and family online. Feel very comfortable about using online tools.			World-class customer service.

65

SEAMLY.CO

Seamly.co is a sustainable apparel company that uses surplus fabrics to produce women's apparel in the USA.

See a full-sized, 8.5x11 version of the Seamly.co case study on www.difference.is

♠ the difference map

CREATED FOR: Seamly.co

DATE:

PRINCIPLES

Truth about me/us

Dedicated to sustainability.

Work with experts in development and production.

Understand the target market.

Experienced in sustainable fashion and marketing.

Truth about the market/industry

Saturated with fast fashion.

Overwhelmingly using cheap and sweatshop labour.

Rife with human-rights issues.

Beset by unsustainable practices (pesticides, GMOs, chemical dumping).

Truth about the people I/we want to serve

Shop for organic fruits and vegetables, but don't know much about sustainable fashion and why it's important.

May not shop online, unless inspired by the offering.

Are willing to spend money on products they believe in.

Generally don't buy into the big fashion marketing machine.

Can't be fooled by trends.

PURPOSE	PEOPLE	PERSONAL	PERCEPTION	PRODUCT
Why do we exist?	**Who is this for? What do they care about?**	**How can we change how people feel? How can we help them live better lives?**	**What do they believe? What would we like them to believe about us?**	**What do people really want or need? How do we create value for our customers?**
To give consumers a reasonably priced alternative to throwaway fashion.	Care about the environment. Want easy, no-fuss style (but always want to look their best).	Provide clarity around fast fashion's ills.	Personal style is paramount.	Comfortable, effortless clothing.
To prove that sustainability and style can exist together—and be financially feasible for the business.	Have disposable income, and want to use their purchasing power on products they believe in.	Showcase our design and production process.	They don't believe in buying something they'll never wear, just to support a cause.	Great fit.
		Offer apparel with great fit, quality, and fabric, and provide superior service.	They believe there is a better way to shop, but maybe haven't found it.	Classic styles, not trend-driven.
To educate the market about human and environmental issues in the fashion industry.	Are avid travellers—on weekends or long-term.	Let our customer's voice be heard as a consumer who actually matters, not as a cog in a commercial machine.	We want our customers to believe that we are the real deal—not greenwashed.	Reasonable price point.
To foster appreciation for the craft of design and sewing amongst our target market.			We want them to believe they really can make a difference by supporting Seamly.co with their dollars.	Multi-use, versatile clothing.

67

CHARITY: WATER

charity: water is a non-profit organization bringing clean and safe drinking water to people in developing nations.

See a full-sized, 8.5x11 version of the charity: water case study on www.difference.is

difference

the difference map

CREATED FOR: charity:water

DATE:

PRINCIPLES

Truth about me/us	**Truth about the market/industry**	**Truth about the people I/we want to serve**
Transparent. Passionate. Committed. Creative problem-solvers who want to make a difference in the world.	Perceived lack of transparency around the impact that donations made to charities actually have in real terms. Mistrust is a challenge facing charities. Every $1 invested in improved water supply and sanitation can yield from $4 to $12 for the local economy, depending on the type of project.	30,000 deaths occur every week from unsafe water and unhygienic living conditions; 90% of those are children under five years old. In Africa alone, people spend 40 billion hours every year walking for water. Women and children usually bear the burden of water collection.

PURPOSE · PEOPLE · PERSONAL · PERCEPTION · PRODUCT

PURPOSE	PEOPLE	PERSONAL	PERCEPTION	PRODUCT
Why do we exist?	**Who is this for? What do they care about?**	**How can we change how people feel? How can we help them live better lives?**	**What do they believe? What would we like them to believe about us?**	**What do people really want or need? How do we create value for our customers?**
To bring clean drinking water to every person in the world.	800 million people have no access to clean drinking water.	Enable donors to start their own campaigns through the 'my charity: water' platform.	There is a mistrust of charities internationally.	A 100% giving model (private donors fund operating costs).
	Women and children spend hours every day walking for water.	With Dollars to Projects, connect donors to the people and projects they are helping.	People worry that the money they donate is spent on operational costs and doesn't reach the people who need it most.	Donation tracking linked to projects.
	Their education suffers because of the need to haul water. Need education to help maintain the wells.	Track donations and link to projects, using GPS, photos and data.	79% of Americans said it's very important to know the percentage of spending that goes towards charitable programs.	Personal fundraising platform. Accountability and transparency, via detailed financials published on the website.
	Are happy to partner with aid organisations to help build infrastructure that will be used once water can be brought to their village.	Create emotional connections with supporters, using storytelling, video, and social media. Share donors' stories.	Only 1 in 10 Americans believe that charities are 'honest and ethical'.	Liaison with experienced partners in the field who help villagers create the infrastructure needed to both introduce and sustain the clean water supply.
			All the money they donate goes directly to the people who need it.	

69

SIMPLE.COM

Simple is reinventing personal banking with modern online and mobile experiences, no surprise fees, and great customer service. The alternative to traditional banking.

See a full-sized, 8.5x11 version of the Simple case study on www.difference.is

difference

♠ the difference map

CREATED FOR: Simple.com

DATE:

PRINCIPLES

Truth about me/us	**Truth about the market/industry**	**Truth about the people I/we want to serve**
Want to be more human and in partnership for our customers.	The industry is designed to make banking work, not for the way people think.	Worry about money.
Launched without focus-group feedback on the product.	Systems were built 20–40 years ago.	Are frustrated with banks.
Creative, caring and passionate.	Websites are built around archaic design choices.	Like to have smooth cash flows; lean on a credit card to fill in the gaps.
Data driven; we measure our impact.	Banking industry profits from keeping people confused.	Want to get on with their lives and have a sense of control over their finances.
Control our own technology.	Tightly regulated political space.	
	Technology involved is complex.	

PURPOSE	PEOPLE	PERSONAL	PERCEPTION	PRODUCT
Why do we exist?	**Who is this for? What do they care about?**	**How can we change how people feel!? How can we help them live better lives?**	**What do they believe? What would we like them to believe about us?**	**What do people really want or need? How do we create value for our customers?**
To make banking awesome by helping people to understand and better control their finances.	People who are dissatisfied with the banking status quo.	Listen to our customers first in an authentic, personal way.	Banks don't have our best interests at heart.	A human-oriented mobile banking application.
	Want to feel empowered, not stupid.	Empower customers with features that help them to know how much money they have (using the Safe-to-Spend feature).	Banking fees are unfair and not transparent.	A simple credit card, with no surprise fees.
	Not rational thinkers about finance; have a lot of emotions about money.	Help people to save (with the Goals feature).	We don't trust banks.	Powerful budgeting and saving tools built right into accounts. All tools accessible via Web, iPhone, and Android.
	Are becoming more comfortable with banking online and via mobile devices.	Make banking more human by putting customer service at the core of everything we do.	Banks don't care about us.	Tools that help them save money and spend it wisely.
			Banks won't respond to my needs.	Banking systems designed for the way people think.
			'I feel like an idiot when I pay an overdraft fee.'	Responsive customer service.
			We are the best bank in the world.	
			Our worry-free alternative to traditional banking helps them make smarter choices.	

71

UBER

Uber, founded in 2009, is a transportation network company that connects passengers with the drivers of cars for hire via a mobile application. Using the application on a smartphone, people can reserve cars and use GPS to track the driver's journey to them. Because payments are also made within the app and processed by Uber, there is no need to carry cash or credit cards. Hirers can also use the app to get a quote for their trip and to give feedback about drivers. Uber takes a percentage of the revenue generated from each hire. The company began life by connecting passengers to the drivers of black Town Cars. The service expanded in 2012 to include a wider range of cars with UberX, to make Uber more accessible to more people.

See a full-sized, 8.5x11 version of the Uber case study on www.difference.is

the difference map

CREATED FOR: Uber

DATE:

PRINCIPLES

Truth about me/us

Creative problem-solvers.

We believe every problem has a solution.

Hard working.

Believe in having fun.

Software engineers and entrepreneurs.

Track record in innovation and scaling entrepreneurial ventures.

Truth about the market/industry

Taxi hire hasn't changed for decades.

There are inefficiencies in time lost across several areas of the taxi hire system.

Keeping people moving around cities is big business.

There are no companies with a dominant market share in this industry.

Taxi and limousine service in the U.S. is a $10 billion industry.

Truth about the people I/we want to serve

People don't like the uncertainty of hiring and waiting for a taxi, and not knowing if their ride will arrive.

Some people will pay a premium for the convenience and certainty.

People place a premium on time.

Drivers often have no reliable way to make direct contact with customers.

PURPOSE	PEOPLE	PERSONAL	PERCEPTION	PRODUCT
Why do we exist?	Who is this for? What do they care about?	How can we change how people feel? How can we help them live better lives?	What do they believe? What would we like them to believe about us?	What do people really want or need? How do we create value for our customers?
To evolve the way the world moves, make cities more accessible and bring people and their cities closer.	People are time poor.	Give the hirer more control over the car hire experience.	Taxis are often unreliable or unavailable at peak times.	A mobile application that connects passengers to drivers in real time via their smartphones.
	They need and expect services that are reliable.	Enable hirers to track and contact their drivers.	'Where is he?'	An app that allows them to track the driver's arrival to their current destination, make secure payments via their phone, and rate the driver at the end of their trip.
	Our customers place a premium on time.	Enable people to hire a car without knowing their exact location.	'Will I get there on time?'	
	Convenience has a real-world value for our customers.	Make the experience seamless by including payment processing within the app.	Passengers worry that they will be overcharged at the end of the journey.	The ability to push a button and get a ride.
	Drivers need more business and a way to connect with customers in real time.	Give drivers the opportunity to take control of, plan and manage their workload.	Meter watching is unnerving.	A seamless experience.
		Include a driver ratings system that allows customers to give feedback.	People would rather know the cost of the hire up front.	
			'Where has this service been all my life?'	

73

USING THE DIFFERENCE MAP: THE TEMPLATE

The Difference Map is designed to help you to recognise opportunities that create both tangible and intangible value, to develop products and services that people want, and to matter to your customers. Now that you've read the case studies and seen how the Difference Map can be used, try it out for yourself. You can use it to design, plan, structure, reimagine, reinvent, market and grow your business.

Instead of beginning your business plan by considering how to sell an existing or new product or service, use the Difference Map to look at principles—fundamental truths—first. Focusing on insights about you, your prospective customers and the market or industry you operate in helps you to understand where the opportunities to innovate and create difference are. Next, consider the reason your business exists, and then the people who are your customers or prospective customers.

The Difference Map works best if it's completed in the following order:

1.   Principles

2.   Purpose

3.   People

4.   Perception

5.   Personal

6.   Product

Ask and answer as many questions as you can for each of the six sections. The questions on the map will get you started, but feel free to add your own.

Download your free copy of the Difference Map from www.difference. is. Print multiples, enlarge them, stick Post-it notes on them, draw on them, scribble on them and share them with your team. Then go make your ideas matter!

THE THING THAT DIFFERENTIATES A GOOD IDEA FROM A GREAT ONE

Actually, what differentiates a good anything from a great anything you care to think about (business, movie, hotel, product, blog, book, packaging, design, app, talk, school, song, art… keep going) is that the great stuff, the things we give a damn about, have the heart left in them.

What do I mean by 'heart'? The empathy and emotion. The feeling, and yes, vulnerability. Yours, not the marketing department's.

Good products work. Great products become part of our story.

A good speaker leaves us with food for thought. A great speaker leaves his heart on the podium.

Good marketing tells the story. Great marketing *is* the story.

We don't just notice or respond to difference; most of the time we can't even explain it.

We simply feel it. We just know.

And that's what makes it matter.

BEING UNDERVALUED VS. BEING 'THE ONE'

Design is undervalued. So is journalism, and song writing, and the guy who wrote the code that made the balls in the app bounce. I can have a logo designed for $249, using 99designs, one of many crowd-sourced design platforms. I'll get thirty designs to choose from, created by various designers, and although many people will dispute this, at least one design will probably be good enough. For many creative professionals, low-priced crowd-sourcing is a problem for sure.

And yet designer and letterer Jessica Hische is sought after; she gets to choose whom she works with and names her price. If I want to apply design thinking to a new innovation, of course I go straight to IDEO because, well, who else would you go to but the best? Nancy Duarte's company designs presentations for people like Al Gore and Bill Gates, and for companies like Twitter and Hewlett-Packard. If you want to shine at TED Global, hiring Duarte is a no-brainer.

Every day, people are being well paid to use the skills you have, not because they are better than you, but because they decided that's what they wanted and they worked towards it. They recognised the truth about their talents, they taught themselves how to see what people really wanted, and they executed with difference.

Should the Samsung CEO spend his day punching his desk, while lamenting the reason we fall in love with anything Apple designs and brings to market every damn time? Or should he just get on and lead the company so that it creates difference for its customers?

The answer is not to sit around imploring the industry or the customer to give us back our value. It's not up to our customers to value us. It's up to us to show them why they should and to do work that creates a difference. There is no more business as usual for musicians, or journalists, or designers, or [insert your profession here because it's sure to be next]. No cushy numbers. No Get Out Of Jail Free card. There is only work that matters.

The way forward for designers, creatives, and maybe you, or your company, is not to be lumped in with the competition. It's to understand the people you want to serve, and why, and then to be 'the one' for them. You must do what it takes not to be just another creative or professional, but to be *the creative or professional* that people who want the particular must have. Jessica Hische and Nancy Duarte made a choice. They decided what they wanted to be the best in the world at helping people to do; then they created difference by doing it. You might not be able to change how the world values your profession, but you *can* change how *you* are valued by doing work that matters. Work that changes how people feel, not just what they think.

We have two choices. We can stand around looking at the train wreck of what was, or we can design our own futures.

Which are you going for?

HOW YOU CREATE DIFFERENCE

> *It's so scary to show up. It feels dangerous to be seen, it's terrifying. But it is not as scary, dangerous or terrifying as getting to the end of our lives and thinking—what if I would have shown up? What would have been different?*
> —Brené Brown

If there's one thing I know from working and speaking with hundreds of business owners, CEOs, brand managers and entrepreneurs over the years, it's this: nobody sets out to be average. In fact, what people want to be is exactly the opposite. As soon as we open our eyes every morning, what we want most is to matter, to live a life and to do work that has meaning. We have evolved to feel this way. Man's first thought was 'I AM'.

And of course once we recognised that, we understood that one day we would not be, and we began to question how to make meaning from what we did, in the time we had. We have evolved to go in search of and live a life that is meaningful. We are hardwired to want to tap into our difference and to bring that difference to the world.

Through the magic of Twitter, I recently asked British writer Ricky Gervais—the creator of some of the most successful TV comedy-dramas of our time, like *The Office* and *Derek*—if there was a universal truth that underpinned his writing, and if so, what that was. His reply: 'Probably that everyone needs love'. It turns out that what applies to creating great drama, good storytelling, and life also applies to business. We sometimes forget that.

In a world where we've seen big brands dominate markets for decades, we could be forgiven for thinking that what people want is more of the same with a twist of lemon. But times have changed; the proof of that is all around us. Every day we see entrepreneurial ventures founded on difference take off and fly, while many of the big brands that have been *Fortune* 500 companies for years—companies like Eastman Kodak and Sears—plummet headlong into the ground.

We are living in a unique moment in time. An age where we can bring things to the world without having to own a factory or an office building. A digital age that gives us more opportunities to really listen and to learn how to see what people are longing for. Through mediums like Twitter and Facebook, it's possible to see how your customers are reacting to the world and to your brand in real time. It's only when we do this with empathy that we can create ideas and brands that matter.

The truth about how people feel and how you can change or influence that for the better is all around you. As I'm writing these last few paragraphs to you from my local café, a smartly dressed, soft-spoken guy in his early thirties is sitting with his colleague opposite, admitting how guilty he felt as he dropped his little girl off at day care just minutes before. Apparently what made it worse was the act of 'taking her out of the car and leaving her there'. Truths, problems and unexpressed desires are all around us waiting to be solved or fulfilled.

You don't have to buy customers, or loyalty and love, with more features, coupons and billboards. You can earn all of this by creating difference. By wanting to bring the thing people will love to them. By mattering to them, maybe even more than their wallet one day.

We were not born to be convinced by things that can be weighed and measured. Our attention can no longer be held by things we don't care about. Somehow we've come to believe that standing out is about being different. The truth is that what really moves us is feelings, not facts. There are a thousand ways for you to get noticed, but there's only one way to really touch someone. And that's to give them a reason to care, a story they can believe in. Great stories are woven, not told. They come to us in whispers, as goose bumps. A wry smile playing on our lips, a vigorous nod, a feeling we can't explain. Or as a number scribbled on the back of a napkin, a shared link accompanied by a message that says, 'you gotta see this', which really means 'I want you to experience this with me'.

We have the power to create things, experiences, connections, moments and stories that change people. We can reimagine what it means to make an impact. We have the opportunity to reinvent the way we do business. Creating difference is a choice and it's yours to make. I hope you do, because it matters.

References

FRONT MATTER

"*"Different" and "new" is relatively easy'* — Helen Walters, 'Jonathan Ive on The Key to Apple's Success', *Bloomberg Businessweek*, 8 July 2009. <http://www.businessweek.com/innovate/next/archives/2009/07/jonathan_ive_th.html>

INTRODUCTION

... *the first prototype of the mouse* — Malcolm Gladwell, 'Creation Myth'. *The New Yorker,* 16 May 2011. <http://www.newyorker.com/reporting/2011/05/16/110516fa_fact_gladwell>

Story about Jobs' reaction to seeing the PARC team's mouse —'BBC Documentary: Steve Jobs - Billion Dollar Hippy.' YouTube, 16 December 2011. <https://www.youtube.com/watch?v=OC3qFtgeogE&gt>

Steve Jobs had other ideas — Malcolm Gladwell, 'Creation Myth'.

The design brief he gave Hovey — 'Steve Jobs - Billion Dollar Hippy'.

The Apple Macintosh was the first mass-market personal computer — 'Macintosh', *Wikipedia*. <https://en.wikipedia.org/wiki/Apple_Macintosh>

Malcolm Gladwell describes Jobs as 'a tweaker' — Malcolm Gladwell, 'The Tweaker: The Real Genius of Steve Jobs'. *The New Yorker,* 14 November 2011. <http://www.newyorker.com/reporting/2011/11/14/111114fa_fact_gladwell>

...devices that would 'make our heart sing' — When Steve Jobs introduced the iPad 2 in 2011, he said, 'It is in Apple's DNA that technology alone is not enough—it's technology married with liberal arts, married with the humanities, that yields us the results that make our heart sing...'. — Jonah Lehrer, 'Steve Jobs: "Technology Alone Is Not Enough"'. *The New Yorker*, 7 October 2011. <http://www.newyorker.com/online/blogs/newsdesk/2011/10/steve-jobs-pixar.html>

Dean Hovey quotes: (1) *Jobs 'connected the dots'* — 'BBC Documentary: Steve Jobs - Billion Dollar Hippy'. (2) *Jobs was 'brilliant at figuring out what a computer ought to be'* — 'Interview with Dean Hovey', *Making the Macintosh: Technology and Culture in Silicon Valley*. <http://www-sul.stanford.edu/mac/primary/interviews/hovey/trans.html>

The invention and adoption of the shopping cart — 'Fascinating facts about the invention of the shopping cart by Sylvan Goldman in 1937', *The Great Idea Finder*. <http://www.ideafinder.com/history/inventions/shopcart.htm>

Neil Blumenthal understood that style mattered — 'Neil Blumenthal: Brand Building Through Narrative & Vulnerability,' PSFK Conference NYC 2013. <http://vimeo.com/66192517>

THE LOST ART OF MARKETING

If you'd lived in Europe during the medieval era — 'Medieval Cuisine'. *Wikipedia*. <http://en.wikipedia.org/wiki/Medieval_cuisine#cite_ref-HM_16_1-0>

A win for Frederick — Jeff Chapman, 'The Impact of the Potato'. *History Magazine, Volume 2*. <http://www.history-magazine.com/potato.html>

... the potato was responsible for a quarter of the growth — Nathan Nunn and Nancy Qian, 'The Potato's Contribution To Population And Urbanization: Evidence From A Historical Experiment'. *Quarterly Journal of Economics* 126.2 (2011): 593-650.

... essentially turning the funnel on its head — Seth Godin, 'The unforgiving arithmetic of the funnel'. *Seth's Blog,* 7 June 2012. <http://sethgodin.typepad.com/seths_blog/2012/06/the-unforgiving-arithmetic-of-the-funnel.html>

The original Marketing Mix — Neil H. Borden, *The Concept of the Marketing Mix.* Cambridge: Harvard Business School, 1984.

'holes in the marketplace' and *'The basic approach to positioning is'* — Al Ries and Jack Trout, *Positioning: The Battle for Your Mind.* New York: McGraw-Hill, 1986.

We spent $500 billion globally on advertising — Ingrid Lunden, 'Digital Ads Will Be 22% Of All U.S. Ad Spend In 2013, Mobile Ads 3.7%; Total Global Ad Spend In 2013 $503B'. *TechCrunch*, 30 September 2013. <http://techcrunch.com/2013/09/30/digital-ads-will-be-22-of-all-u-s-ad-spend-in-2013-mobile-ads-3-7-total-gobal-ad-spend-in-2013-503b-says-zenithoptimedia/>

Definition of 'advertise' — Dictionary.com. <http://mfeed.reference.com/d/search.html?q=advertiser>

Pampers' USP and Pampers vs. Huggies — 'Pampers'. *Contagious Magazine,* Feb. 2011: 1–12.

'People tell us who they are' — 'The Summer Man,' *Mad Men*, season 4, *Don Draper Quotes*. <http://www.amctv.com/shows/mad-men/cast/don-draper>

... growing the company by 500 percent — Eric Markowitz, 'How Warby Parker Grew So Fast: 3 Reasons'. *Inc.com,* 7 March 2012 <http://www.inc.com/eric-markowitz/3-reasons-warby-parker-is-killing-it.html>

'Although many of us may think of ourselves' — Jill Bolte Taylor, *My Stroke of Insight: A Brain Scientist's Personal Journey*. New York: Viking, 2008.

Gerald Zaltman says that 95 percent of our decision-making — Manda Mahoney, 'The Subconscious Mind of the Consumer (And How To Reach It)'. *HBS Working Knowledge,* 13 January 2003. <http://hbswk.hbs.edu/item/3246.html>

LEARNING HOW TO SEE

'self-described 'MIT bike geeks' — 'Our Story', Fortified Bicycle Alliance. <http://fortifiedbike.com/pages/bicycle-light>

The founders 'followed them on rainy night-time commutes' — Slava Menn, 'Want To Fund Your Kickstarter? You're Not Steve Jobs—Ask People What They Want'. *Co.Exist,* 16 October 2013. <http://www.fastcoexist.com/3020068/want-to-fund-your-kickstarter-youre-not-steve-jobs-ask-people-what-they-want?>

The Fortified Bike Alliance team created a light — Slava Menn, 'Fortified: Bike Lights That Last Forever. We Promise.' Kickstarter. <http://www.kickstarter.com/projects/gotham/fortified-bike-lights-that-last-forever-we-promise >

TINY MARKETS OF SOMEONE

The bell curve has melted — 'Seth Godin on Sculpting the Future - Further with Ford'. YouTube, 10 July 2013. <http://www.youtube.com/watch?v=xkMZq_DJYvI&feature=youtu.be>

Chobani went from having almost no revenue — Bryan Gruley, 'At Chobani, the Turkish King of Greek Yogurt'. *Bloomberg Businessweek,* 31 January 2013. <http://www.businessweek.com/articles/2013-01-31/at-chobani-the-turkish-king-of-greek-yogurt>

'a centuries-old technique of straining to remove excess liquid' — Chobani Greek Yogurt FAQ, <http://chobani.com/products/faq/>.

He wanted to make Greek yogurt — 'Chobani Founder and CEO Hamdi Ulukaya Named Ernst & Young World Entrepreneur Of The Year 2013'. *PR Newswire*, 10 June 2013. <http://www.prnewswire.com/news-releases/chobani-founder-and-ceo-hamdi-ulukaya-named-ernst--young-world-entrepreneur-of-the-year-2013-210806821.html>

Airbnb went from appealing to people at the edges — 'Airbnb: 10 Million Guest Nights Booked', Airbnb. <https://www.airbnb.com/10-million?cdn_locale_redirect=1>.

Method achieved over 500 percent growth — 'Method Products'. *Inc.com.* <http://www.inc.com/profile/method-products>

BUILDING YOUR BRAND ONE PERSON AT A TIME

The Rubik's Cube became the best-selling puzzle toy — George Webster, 'The little cube that changed the world'. CNN, 11 October 2012. <http://www.cnn.com/2012/10/10/tech/rubiks-cube-inventor/>

PEOPLE DON'T BUY FEATURES; THEY BUY PROMISES

The fortune, not the cookie — Bernadette Jiwa, *The Fortune Cookie Principle: The 20 Keys to a Great Brand Story and Why Your Business Needs One.* Australia: The Story of Telling Press, 2013.

THINKING BEYOND CUSTOMER NEEDS

the 40 percent of customers who bought McDonald's milkshakes — Clayton Christensen, Scott Cook, and Taddy Hall, 'What Customers Want from Your Products'. *HBS Working Knowledge,* 16 January 2006 <http://hbswk.hbs.edu/item/5170.html>. Additional information from Derek Christensen, 'Hiring Milkshakes (and other secrets to product development)'. Derekchristensen.com. <http://www.derekchristensen.com/hiring-milkshakes-and-other-secrets-to-product-development/>

EMOTIONAL POINTS OF DIFFERENCE

Singapore's Changi Airport — 'Changi Airport Singapore: Facts & Statistics'. <http://www.changiairport.com/our-business/about-changi-airport/facts-statistics>

WHAT YOU MEASURE MATTERS, BUT WHAT'S HARD TO MEASURE MIGHT MATTER MORE

'When return on investment is measured by delight' — Lain Shakespeare, 'The Story Behind the MailChimp Billboards'. MailChimp Blog, 3 December 2012. <http://blog.mailchimp.com/the-story-behind-the-mailchimp-billboards/>

DEMOGRAPHICS VS. WORLDVIEWS

'a growing class of high-value consumers' and *'have progressive social and political attitudes'* — Ross Honeywill, The NEO Group. <http://www.neogroup.net/ABOUT/Background/tabid/140/Default.aspx> and <http://www.neogroup.net/NEOs/tabid/74/Default.aspx>

'consumer behaviour is largely predictable' — Chris Norton and Ross Honeywill, *One Hundred Thirteen Million Markets of One: How The New Economic Order Can Remake The American Economy.* Fingerprint Strategies Inc., 2012.

THE DIFFERENCE MODEL

'The notion of empathy and human-centeredness' — David Kelley and Tom Kelley, *Creative Confidence: Unleashing the Creative Potential Within Us All.* New York: Crown Business, 2013.

'If you want to make something new' — Seth Godin, 'Learning how to see'. *Seth's Blog,* 25 December 2012. <http://sethgodin.typepad.com/seths_blog/2012/12/learning-how-to-see.html>

'he wanted to create something that was so instrumental' — Andrew Wray, 'Former Apple manager tells how the original iPhone was developed, why it went with Gorilla Glass'. *iMore,* 4 February 2012. <http://www.imore.com/apple-manager-tells-original-iphone-born>

The founders of MOO.com knew back in 2004 — 'About MOO'. <http://uk.moo.com/about/history.html>

Spanx founder Sara Blakely — Spanx, 'About Us'. <http://www.spanx.com/-cms-page.aboutus?ab=footer_About%20SPANX%>.

The fifty top performing brands — Bernadette Jiwa, *The Fortune Cookie Principle.*

When Jane Ní Dhulchaointigh invented Sugru — sugru, 'A partial visual history of sugru'. <http://sugru.com/story>

'But increasingly companies around the globe' — Jan Chipchase and Simon Steinhardt, *Hidden in Plain Sight: How to Create Extraordinary Products for Tomorrow's Customers.* New York: HarperBusiness, 2013.

The founders of Dollar Shave Club — Dollar Shave Club, 'How it Works.' <https://www.dollarshaveclub.com/how-it-works>

'We see our customers as invited guests' — Doug Meyer, 'Staying in Touch with Your Customers'. *Corp!,* 5 August 2010. <http://www.corpmagazine.com/executives-entrepreneurs/entrepreneurs/itemid/1723/staying-in-touch-with-your-customers>

For every pair of shoes they sell — TOMS Company Overview, <http://www.toms.com/corporate-info/l>.

'Our personal beliefs define our choices' — Tom Asacker, *The Business of Belief: How the World's Best Marketers, Designers, Salespeople, Coaches, Fundraisers, Educators, Entrepreneurs and Other Leaders Get Us to Believe.* CreateSpace, 2013.

The Little Veggie Patch Co. in Melbourne —The Little Veggie Patch Co. <http://littleveggiepatchco.com.au/>

'Make something people want' — Paul Graham, 'Be Good'. *PaulGraham.com,* 1 April 2008. <http://www.paulgraham.com/good.html>

'people who 'just wanted to push a button and get a ride' — Andy Kessler, 'Travis Kalanick: The Transportation Trustbuster'. *The Wall*

Street Journal, 25 January 2013, <http://online.wsj.com/news/articles/
SB10001424127887324235104578244231122376480>. Additional
information about Uber from these sources: (1) Nicholas Jackson,
'Hailing a Cab With Your Phone'. *The Atlantic*, 16 November 1020,
<http://www.theatlantic.com/technology/archive/2010/11/hailing-
a-cab-with-your-phone/66630/>; and (2) Joshua Brustein, 'The
Smartphone Way to Beckon a Car'. *The New York Times*, 16 May 2011,
<http://www.nytimes.com/2011/05/15/nyregion/uber-and-weeels-
offer-car-services-by-phone-app.html>

THE DIFFERENCE MODEL: CASE STUDIES

The market for gluten-free products — Jefferson Adams, 'Gluten-
Free Products Market to Top 6.2 Billion by 2018'.*Celiac.com*, 5 August
2013. <http://www.celiac.com/articles/23336/1/Global-Gluten-Free-
Products-Market-to-Top-62-Billion-by-2018/Page1.html]>

MOO set out to 'disrupt the $100 billion global print industry…' —
'About Moo'. <http://us.moo.com/about/history.html>.

Sugru is 'a self-setting rubber…' — 'What is sugru?' <http://sugru.
com/about>.

Information about Warby Parker — from Khari Parson, 'Fireside
chat with Dave Gilboa'.*Startup Grind*, 21 October 2013.<http://
startupgrind.com/2013/10/fireside-chat-with-dave-gilboa-co-
founder-and-co-ceo-of-warby-parker/>

Travel and tourism industry's total contribution — 'Travel &
Tourism larger industry than automotive manufacturing'. World
Travel & Tourism Council, 18 April 2012.<http://www.wttc.org/news-
media/news-archive/2012/travel-tourism-larger-industry-automotive-
manufacturing/>

79% of Americans said... — Lukas O. Berg, 'The Trust Report'. Charity Star, October 2011. <http://www.charitystar.org/wp-content/uploads/2011/05/The-Trust-Report1.pdf>

Simple is reinventing personal banking — 'Josh Reich: People Say They Need Complexity, But What They Want Is Simplicity'. *99U*. <http://99u.com/videos/20233/josh-reich-design-is-not-a-department>

There are no companies with a dominant market share— 'Taxi & Limousine Services in the US: Market Research Report.' *IBISWorld*, August 2013. <http://www.ibisworld.com/industry/default.aspx?indid=1951>

BEING UNDERVALUED VS. BEING 'THE ONE'

So is journalism — Tim Kreider, 'Slaves of the Internet, Unite!' *New York Times*, 26 October 2013. <http://www.nytimes.com/2013/10/27/opinion/sunday/slaves-of-the-internet-unite.html?pagewanted=1&_r=2>

designer and letterer Jessica Hische — Jessica's website is <http://jessicahische.is/awesome/>.

Nancy Duarte's company designs presentations — See some of Nancy Duarte's work at <http://www.duarte.com/portfolio/>.

HOW YOU CREATE DIFFERENCE

'It's so scary to show up' — 'Brené Brown: Why Your Critics Aren't The Ones Who Count', <http://99u.com/videos/20052/brene-brown-stop-focusing-on-your-critics>.

Man's first thought was 'I AM' — Ernest Holmes, *The Science of Mind*. Wilder Publications, 2007.

***...many of the big brands that have been Fortune 500 companies* —**
Brian Solis, *What's the Future of Business? Changing the Way Businesses
Create Experiences.* Hoboken, N.J.: Wiley, 2013. Additional information
from Rick Newman, '10 Great Companies that Lost Their Edge'. *U.S.
News & World Report,* 19 August 2010. <http://money.usnews.com/
money/blogs/flowchart/2010/08/19/10-great-companies-that-lost-
their-edge>

Acknowledgements

It's said that it takes a village to raise a child. I think the same applies to birthing a book. Putting our ideas 'out there' in ink and pixels is scary. It turns out that the act of doing just that—of not allowing yourself, as Brené Brown says, to be defined by what critics think—enables you to stop playing small. You need a great team around you to hold your hand, to question, to have your back and to push you on the days you don't feel like pushing yourself because fear is standing in your way. And you need people to love you whatever happens. I am lucky to have all of those people to thank.

Thank YOU for reading my blog and buying this book. I hope it starts, or keeps you on, the journey to creating your difference. Without you, there would be no reason to write.

Thank you to all of the businesses and entrepreneurs featured in the book for giving me stories to tell. Your work inspires me every day.

Thanks to Reese Spykerman, who understands how to create difference and connection through design. She's done it again! Thanks to my editor, Catherine Oliver, for being the perfect dance partner. The job of an editor is damned hard. Catherine nails it.

Thanks to Porter Jamison for being an excellent proof-reader and second set of eyes.

Thanks to my friend Kelly Exeter, for jumping on her white charger at the eleventh hour.

To my friend David McKinney, thanks for helping me to get these ideas out of my head amongst the salt cellars and coffee cups.

Thanks as always to Seth Godin for not letting me off the hook, for generous scepticism and a level gaze that says, 'You can; you just have to decide'. I also have Seth to thank for breaking the section on the characteristics of difference thinkers as only he knows how.

To my three boys for keeping my feet on the ground, for rolling their eyes, for making me laugh at myself and for letting me know what really matters.

To Moyez, for love and weekend walks and for encouraging me to be brave and not to play small no matter what.

Where to from here?

My hope is that this is more than a book. I'd like it to be the beginning of a conversation about how we can get better at building businesses that matter by creating difference for our customers. The truth is there is no modern-day Donald Draper who can save a business from being average, no tagline that will take something from mediocre to significant. The job of every entrepreneur, innovator and marketer going forward is not to ask customers to notice us. Our job is to really see them. We can get better at doing that by sharing our experiences with each other.

I plan to continue adding Difference Map case studies to the book's website at www.difference.is. Please feel free to share your completed Difference Map with me at hello@thestoryoftelling.com. I can't promise to publish every one I receive, but I'll do my best.

You can also keep in touch through my blog at www.TheStoryofTelling.com and on Twitter: @bernadettejiwa.

Made in the USA
San Bernardino, CA
06 March 2014